100 Catholic Things to Do Before You Die

100 Catholic Things to Do Before You Die

Earl J. Higgins

PELICAN PUBLISHING COMPANY
GRETNA 2019

*In memory of my wife, Janet
devout and compassionate healer*

Library of Congress Cataloging-in-Publication Data

Names: Higgins, Earl J., author.
Title: 100 Catholic things to do before you die / Earl J. Higgins.
Other titles: One hundred Catholic things to do before you die
Description: Gretna : Pelican Publishing Company, 2019. |
    Includes index.
Identifiers: LCCN 2018048171| ISBN 9781455623686 (pbk. :
    alk. paper) | ISBN 9781455623693 (ebook)
Subjects: LCSH: Catholic Church--Customs and practices.
Classification: LCC BX1754 .H5195 2019 | DDC 282--dc23 LC
    record available at https://lccn.loc.gov/2018048171

All images from the Library of Congress unless otherwise noted

Printed in the United States of America

Published by Pelican Publishing Company, Inc.
1000 Burmaster Street, Gretna, Louisiana 70053
www.pelicanpub.com

Contents

Introduction to the Catholic Bucket List

In the name of the Father and of the Son and of the Holy Spirit. Amen.

You're Catholic, right? Catholics begin *everything* with the Sign of the Cross. It is not just an affirmation of belief in the Holy Trinity; it is a verbal connection to God. Catholics begin the day with it, getting out of bed for quick morning prayer. It is said before saying grace before meals. Mass begins with the Sign of the Cross. It is made before falling asleep.

Athletes make the Sign of the Cross while standing at bat at home plate, before shooting a foul shot, after scoring a touchdown. Parents make the Sign of the Cross over their children at emotional and wrenching life moments, such as the first day of school, driving the car for the first time, departing on a first date. It invokes a blessing at leaving-home events, with all the anxiety that accompanies those markers of human progression: summer camp; high school graduation; joining the military, the Peace Corps, or other form of far-off public service; graduation from college; getting married.

The Sign of the Cross is an integral part of the ceremony of Baptism, with both the parents and the godparents making the sign on the forehead of the person being baptized.

Catholics also make the Sign of the Cross in times of perceived danger: approaching storms, a journey along a treacherous route, and when a vague sense of the presence of evil creates a physical response that will chase the evil spirits away.

At the burial site of a loved one, Catholics make the Sign of the Cross to help the deceased achieve eternal happiness and to let them know that they are remembered.

It is appropriate, then, to begin a Catholic "bucket list"—everything a Catholic should do before others say prayers at his or her funeral—with the signature acknowledgment of Catholicism:

In the name of the Father and of the Son and of the Holy Spirit. Amen.

Put some holy water in the bucket, and get started.

1. Start the Liturgical Year with an Advent Wreath

Jesus is coming! His birthday is December 25. Get ready. When does the Christmas season begin? The retail industry starts the season in the early autumn. After Labor Day, signs of commercial Christmas appear, and full sales mode begins as soon as Halloween and All Saints Day pass. By the day after Thanksgiving, "Black Friday," commercial Christmas is in high gear. Catholicism, however, starts the season with Advent, a word meaning "coming," an anticipation of the birth of Jesus. The church's liturgical year begins with Advent.

Start the year with an Advent wreath in your home or church or both. The wreaths can be made at home or purchased. Many department stores, not just Catholic stores, sell Advent wreaths; they are available online. The wreath consists of a ring of greenery like a Christmas wreath, but instead of red holly berries or Christmas décor, the Advent wreath has holders for four candles. The candles represent the four Sundays in Advent and are the colors of the liturgical garb worn by priests on those Sundays. The first, second, and fourth Sundays are purple, and the third Sunday is pink,

although many clerics prefer the term "rose." Purple represents the solemnity of preparation for the birth of Jesus, and pink/rose is for *Gaudete* ("Rejoice") Sunday. One candle is lighted on the first Sunday, two candles on the Second Sunday, and so forth.

As the Advent wreath is blessed before Mass on the first Sunday, it is the time to chant the familiar Advent hymn "O Come, O Come, Emmanuel." Advent is also the time for some traditional Advent prayers to be said individually or while lighting the candles in the home before a family meal.

It is often a challenge to get the first-lighted candle to last the entire season because it is burned whenever the wreath is lighted. A nub of a candle is no less devotional than a tall one. It's the spirit that counts; Jesus is coming. The devotion of the Advent wreath gets Catholics in the right frame of mind to celebrate Christmas. Remember: it's Jesus' birthday that is coming, not Santa Claus's.

2. Display a "Keep Christ in Christmas" Bumper Sticker

The Knights of Columbus and other Catholic devotional and service organizations annually sponsor the display of signs, magnets, banners, and bumper stickers to remind all what Christmas is about. The slogan is seen on vehicles, in yards, and on commercial billboards, as well as in front of churches and Catholic schools. The slogan seems to have originated with members of the Lutheran Church in the 1920s, although it has been enthusiastically adopted by Catholics for decades.

The slogan is a reminder to Catholics and all Christians that the purpose of the Christmas season is to celebrate the birth of Jesus. ("Jesus Is the Reason for the Season.") It has been used, however, as an aggressive "in your face" thrust at those who for whatever reason do not associate Christmas with Jesus. Thus it can be a riposte in the perceived "war on Christmas" by those who consider the greeting "Happy Holidays" rather than "Merry Christmas" a slap at the celebration of Christ's birth.

The true spirit of Christmas should be open to compassion and understanding for all, and the slogan should remind Catholics to look inward to their own attitudes and compassion or lack thereof.

The purpose of the Advent season is to prepare oneself spiritually for the reception of Jesus into the world. Using the slogan "Keep Christ in Christmas" as a sort of cultural and theological bludgeon does not mesh with that spirit.

Display a bumper sticker, car magnet, or yard sign for the Christmas season and use it as a reminder to keep an open heart and mind in order to receive the love of Christ.

Another Advent bumper sticker: "Jesus is coming. Look busy."

3. Recite the Christmas Anticipation Prayer

Sometimes called the St. Andrew's Christmas Novena or just the Christmas novena, this prayer is not a novena at all. It is not a nine-day spiritual exercise, nor is it said only nine times. Beginning on the Feast of St. Andrew the Apostle, November 30, the prayer is recited *fifteen* times a day, every day until Christmas, a total of twenty-five days. This means that, to offer the prayer correctly, it must be said fifteen times twenty-five times, 375 separate utterances. By December 24, you should be able to recite it while sleeping. It is said that completing this devotion in full will ensure that God will grant the favor requested. Here it is, full of elegant, old-fashioned, flowery language:

> Hail and blessed be the hour and the moment in which the Son of God was born of the most pure Virgin Mary, at midnight, in Bethlehem, in the piercing cold. In that hour vouchsafe, I beseech Thee, O God, to hear my prayer and grant my desires: (here mention your request). Through the merits of Our Savior Jesus Christ and of the Blessed Mother. Amen.

Why fifteen? Why begin on St. Andrew's Day and not the first Sunday of Advent, the official beginning of the season? And how did the composer of the prayer determine the weather

in Bethlehem two thousand years ago when Jesus was born? And birth at midnight? There's no birth certificate. And just what does "vouchsafe" mean? Ignore these impertinent questions and open your heart and mind to God. Christmas is coming.

4. Know the Doctrine of the Immaculate Conception

The Catholic Church observes December 8 as the Feast of the Immaculate Conception. Many non-Catholics and lots of Catholics too are confused about this holy day. It does *not* mark the conception of Jesus; that event is memorialized in the Feast of the Annunciation, March 25, exactly nine months before Christmas. The Immaculate Conception, rather, is that of Mary, the mother of Jesus. Catholic Church doctrine is that Mary was so special because she was to be the Mother of God that, when she was conceived, her soul was created by God completely free of original sin, unlike the rest of humanity who are born into sin. Thus her soul was from conception "immaculate," spotless, unmarked by sin. The Church celebrates Mary's birthday on September 8, nine months after her Immaculate Conception. Although Mary's conception without original sin was special and mystical, the church calendar recognizes natural, nine-month gestation like all other human beings. The same goes for Jesus.

In the Eastern Orthodox tradition, Mary is called the "Theotokos," the "God-bearer," indicating how theologically significant she is. Being sinless was considered necessary for Mary to accept the role of the Mother of God.

Although this doctrine of the Immaculate Conception of Mary was for hundreds of years a general belief throughout Catholicism, it was not until 1854 that Pope Pius IX declared it to be an official dogma of the Roman Catholic Church. After the pope declared the doctrine, the American Catholic bishops dedicated the United States of America to Mary as the country's patron saint in her title of the Immaculate Conception. The National Shrine in Washington, D.C., is dedicated to Mary, the Immaculate Conception.

All Catholics should know the significance of the doctrine of the Immaculate Conception and be able to explain it to those who may be confused, including other Catholics.

5. Pray to Our Lady of Guadalupe

In 1531, the Holy Mother appeared to a Mexican Indian, Juan Diego, at a place that would become part of Villa de Guadalupe, and she spoke to him in Nahuatl, his native language. She spoke to him of her love for the native people and asked him to go to the bishop and request that a church be built on the site where she appeared so that ordinary Mexicans could come to pray and feel her love. The bishop was skeptical and asked Juan Diego for proof of the apparition. He went back to where he had seen Mary, and she again appeared, telling him to go to a nearby hill

and pick roses. He picked the flowers and wrapped them in his tilma, a type of poncho. When he brought the flowers to the bishop, an image of Our Lady had been imprinted on his tilma. The image was of a dark-skinned woman, identifying her with the native Mexicans.

The apparition and the image were authenticated by the Vatican, and *Nuestra Señora de Guadalupe* became the patron saint of Mexico and all of the Americas. Juan Diego's miraculous garment is displayed in the church built on the site. Our Lady of Guadalupe is a powerful image of the identity of Latin Americans but especially the people of Mexico. The shrine of Guadalupe is a focal point in Mexican culture as well as religion. Hundreds of pilgrims visit the shrine in the heart of Mexico City every day.

Are you planning a vacation, something more exotic than the mountains or the seashore? You would do well to visit Mexico City, a huge, cosmopolitan, and vibrant metropolis, and include in the trip a personal pilgrimage to the shrine. If such a journey is not possible, then on her feast day, December 12, you should visit one of the many churches throughout the United States dedicated to Our Lady of Guadalupe, and pray for inspiration from the patroness of the Americas.

"*Nuestra Señora de Guadalupe, ruega por nosotros.*" You can say it in English too; she'll understand. "Our Lady of Guadalupe, pray for us."

6. Construct an Accurate Nativity Scene

As Christmas approaches, it seems that everybody puts a nativity scene somewhere. They are in homes, in yards, in businesses, and—oh, yes—in Catholic churches. People who aren't Christian erect nativity scenes to be festive and in the spirit of the season. After all, the story of Jesus' birth in a stable is both familiar and touching, not to mention of great theological significance. Any Catholic family that doesn't have a crèche in the home somewhere during the Christmas season might be considered to be dwellers in the realm of "bah, humbug."

The nativity scenes all have a great similarity, without consideration of the scriptural and historical significance. The

wooden shed, the fair-skinned statues, the snow would make someone ignorant of the biblical story think that Jesus was born in northern Europe. Mary kneels, dressed in blue and white, looking serene and well rested. A brand-new mother would probably be on her back or at least sitting down, exhausted after several hours of labor. Speaking of labor, no nativity scene includes a statue of someone who must have been there to ensure a smooth and safe birth: a midwife. In fact, most crib scenes are all-male, with the exception of Mary. There are shepherds and Magi and Joseph and Jesus, all male. Where are the women who must have been there to help bring Baby Jesus into the world?

The Gospel says that the infant Jesus was laid in a manger, an old French word for a trough or bin where animals' feed is placed. Where did the animals eat while Jesus was occupying their food tray?

Here's the challenge to Catholics: construct a nativity scene for your home or yard that looks more like Palestine than Europe, and populate it with more accurate figures. You could have Mary in repose, holding her son, while the midwife and other women stand by with the cloths and water basins that must have been used. You'll get a lot of attention.

7. Attend Christmas Midnight Mass

The shopping is done, the tree is decorated, the parties have been given and attended. Then December 24 arrives. Christmas is tomorrow, and it is a holy day. Christmas Vigil Mass was nearly unknown in days of yore. Very popular now, especially for bringing children to church, Masses on the evening of December 24 were not so long ago not on the calendar. The first opportunity to attend Christmas Mass was at midnight. The old rules required Catholics to abstain from consuming anything, even water, after midnight in order to receive Holy Communion the next morning. That meant that any food and beverages consumed at a party or family event after midnight precluded receiving the Eucharist on Christmas morning.

But observant Catholics could eat and drink up till Mass time, midnight, and still go to communion because the rule could be legally observed. Midnight Mass was a popular social as well as spiritual event then, but many churches no longer schedule Christmas midnight Mass. Because of the availability of Vigil Masses and because the abstinence requirement is virtually eliminated, there are no legalistic incentives to attend Mass at midnight. Pope Benedict XIV, fatigued by age and work, celebrated midnight Mass at St. Peter's Basilica at 10:00 P.M., Rome time. He probably figured it was already midnight somewhere in the world.

Nevertheless, attending Christmas midnight Mass is something every Catholic should do at least once in life. It is especially moving when celebrated in a grand cathedral with choir and organ and an hour or so of caroling in the church before Mass. The drama and solemnity remind the faithful that Christmas is about more than Rudolph and Frosty the Snowman and eggnog.

8. Celebrate Epiphany with King Cake

January 6 is the traditional date of the Feast of the Epiphany, the celebration of the first revelation of Jesus to the Gentiles. Only the Gospel of Matthew writes of the mysterious visitors, and they are identified in various translations as "astrologers," "wise men," "Magi," "from the East." The number is not mentioned, nor are they identified as "kings." The Gospel says that the visitors brought gold, frankincense, and myrrh, thus providing the basis for the tradition that there were three of them and that their rich gifts could have been brought only by wealthy kings. They have been given names by tradition: Gaspar, Melchior, Balthazar. This is an important feast day because it shows that Jesus had come as savior for everybody, not just the Jews.

The Epiphany is also called Twelfth Night because it is twelve days after Christmas and ends the Christmas season. Catholics can observe the day by eating a traditional king cake, a brioche in which is embedded a tiny figure of a child. The child represents the infant Jesus, and cake-eaters must be careful lest they bite down on Baby Jesus and break a tooth. The king cake tradition is identified with New Orleans and Louisiana Catholicism, but it is much older, coming to America from France, where the pastry is called *galette des rois* (cake of the kings).

Catholics don't have to go to France or New Orleans for a king cake, although that may be a good excuse for a winter vacation. If local bakeries don't make king cake, there are packaged mixes and recipes available.

There is a national park named for the day. Point Reyes National Seashore in California was named by a Spanish explorer on January 6, 1603, the day the peninsula was sighted. The Spanish name *La Punta de los Reyes* (The Point of the Kings) became a mixture of Spanish and English, Point Reyes. A picnic after Mass at Point Reyes on January 6 with a king cake would make the day complete.

9. Observe Candlemas

February 2 may be best known as Groundhog Day, but there is an ancient Catholic celebration that day, Candlemas, the Feast of the Candles. Catholic churches burn many candles during the year, and Candlemas is the day on which all those candles are blessed. The blessing of candles on February 2 is not as widely observed as it once was, partly because that date is also the commemoration of the presentation of the infant Jesus in the temple, forty days after his birth, an important Jewish ritual. Also observed on the Catholic calendar on February 2 is the Purification of Mary, another Jewish ritual required of new mothers, that they be "purified" after giving birth.

Catholics bring to Mass on Candlemas their own household candles, those lighted in the advent wreath and to accompany special family prayers. On Candlemas, the household candles will be blessed along with those used in church. By participating in the ritual, Catholics connect with the earliest days of Christianity and the proclamation that Jesus is the light of the world.

February 2 is a busy day. In addition to Candlemas, the Feasts of the Purification of Mary and the Presentation of the Infant Jesus, and Groundhog Day, it is the ancient Celtic observance of Imbolc, a midwinter celebration of light and of hope for spring. Astronomically, February 2 is a cross-quarter day, halfway between the darkness of the winter solstice and the arrival of spring at the equinox. It is easy to see how Candlemas connects to this observance, because the blessed candles will provide light for the rest of the year as the days grow longer until the summer solstice and then begin to shorten again.

10. Light a Votive Candle

At the rear of many Catholic churches are banks of candles in glass cups, arranged in rows on a stand. Some of the cups glow red when the candle is lighted, some are blue, some are clear. These candles are usually called "votive candles," meaning that they burn in fulfillment of a vow. The burning of votive candles is an ancient devotion manifesting a desire to offer something physical and concrete to God, not just a prayer that is abstract and mental. The faithful who light the candles do so in conjunction with a prayer of petition, asking for a favor or blessing from God; or a prayer of thanksgiving for a petition that has been granted or for some important, favorable event; or simply as an act of worship, an acknowledgment of the presence and majesty of the Creator.

The flame and the red color are sometimes associated with the Sacred Heart of Jesus, depicted in art by an image of the Lord holding his chest open to reveal his heart in flames, symbolic of his intense love for everyone. The blue votive candles are usually used as offerings and prayers to Mary, blue being the color most frequently associated with her.

Votive candles are not limited to the rear of the church. They are burned at home for the same reasons. They are placed on personal shrines in yards and waysides and on special occasions when the favor of God or thanks therefor is appropriate. In some places votive candles are placed on the graves of loved ones, asking the Lord to welcome the deceased into a blessed eternity.

Light a votive candle with an accompanying prayer as you leave church. The candle will acknowledge your prayer for hours.

11. Receive a Blessing on St. Blaise's Day

The day after Candlemas, the candles come out again. St. Blaise's Day is February 3, and on that day Catholics get their throats blessed with the candles that were blessed at Mass on Candlemas. St. Blaise is the patron saint of those afflicted with diseases and disorders of the throat. The saint's protection is also sought from choking and strangling—anything that could affect the throat, the windpipe, and the vocal chords.

The legend of St. Blaise is that he was a physician who became bishop of Sebaste in Armenia early in the fourth century. There was persecution of Christians at that time and place, and Blaise sought refuge in a cave. There he performed a miracle, the cure of a young boy who had a fish bone lodged in his throat and was gagging, choking, and having great difficulty breathing. Long before Dr. Heimlich invented his squeeze-the-diaphragm maneuver, Blaise dislodged the fish bone and saved the boy. Possibly his reputation as a healer gave him away, and the Roman authorities arrested and imprisoned him. The mother of the boy he had healed brought food and candles to him in jail, which began the tradition of the connection of Blaise and candles.

Blaise was tortured and beheaded for being a Christian, and his martyrdom began his devotional cult, which grew and became fixed in Christian practice. Today, Catholics and other Christians can receive a blessing after Mass on St. Blaise's Day with two crossed candles (unlit, of course) held under the chin while a special prayer to St. Blaise is recited for healing and for protection from throat diseases and the trauma of choking.

Don't get all choked up. Get your blessing from St. Blaise.

12. Let the Good Times Roll on Mardi Gras

What?! Mardi Gras is Catholic? Despite the holiday's exaggerated reputation for general debauchery, Mardi Gras has its origin in the Catholic institution of Lent. Lent begins on Ash Wednesday, the season of preparation for Easter. It is a time of reflection, prayer, fasting, and abstinence from meat. The no-meat practice is where Mardi Gras, which means "Fat Tuesday" in French, gets its name. It is the day before Ash Wednesday. Mardi Gras is a day of partying and feasting on foods that are to be avoided during Lent.

Another name for Mardi Gras is "Carnival," although that word has become more generic and is applied to many different celebrations. The origin of that word is the Latin phrase *carne vale* (CAR-NAY VA-LAY), meaning "farewell to meat." Eat, drink, and be merry. Tomorrow is Ash Wednesday.

Mardi Gras is observed in many Catholic places around the world, not just the well-publicized and popular celebrations in Rio de Janeiro and New Orleans. In fact, the oldest Mardi

Gras celebration in the United States began in Mobile, Alabama, where it is still joyously observed.

Although a journey—one can hardly call a trip to celebrate Mardi Gras a pilgrimage—to observe Carnival with throngs of festive participants could be on one's bucket list, it can be observed far away by holding a house party or a community gathering.

There are many films about Mardi Gras, some good, some so-so, some pretty bad. For those not in or near a community publicly celebrating the holiday, the night before Ash Wednesday could be an occasion to watch one or more of those movies. *Mardi Gras* (1958), starring Pat Boone, is squeaky-clean, family-friendly. *Easy Rider* (1969), with Dennis Hopper and Peter Fonda, is a cult classic of the counter-culture of that decade. One of the best Mardi Gras films is *Orpheu Negro* ("Black Orpheus") (1959), made in Brazil. It uses the ancient Greek myth of Orpheus and Eurydice in a contemporary setting at *Carnaval* in Rio de Janeiro. Dark and with great music, it tells a compelling story of life and death.

As Mardi Gras revelers say in Louisiana, *"Laissez les bons temps rouler!"* (Let the good times roll!)

13. Fast on Ash Wednesday

No meat today. Lent begins on Ash Wednesday, a time of sacrifice, repentance, and spiritual reflection. The masks, costumes, and strings of beads are put away. This is the day during which Catholics acknowledge their mortality and begin to prepare spiritually for Holy Week and the apex celebration of Christianity, the Resurrection of Jesus. Ash Wednesday usually occurs around the middle to late winter, a good time to reflect on one's life and anticipate a new beginning in Easter and springtime.

The signature event of Ash Wednesday is going to Mass and having ashes marked on one's forehead in the shape of the cross. By the time the priest or other minister has marked a lot of the faithful, his thumb is so covered with ashes that the cross mark doesn't come out clearly. No matter. The spiritual effect is the same, expressed in the words "Remember that you are dust and to dust you shall return." This sentiment is a somber reminder following the colorful gaiety of Mardi Gras.

Fasting and abstinence are integral to Ash Wednesday and all of Lent. Church rules require Catholics to abstain from meat on Ash Wednesday and on all Fridays in Lent. Fasting, which means only one full meal and two smaller meals, is required on Ash Wednesday and Good Friday. No snacking is allowed.

A Lenten devotional tradition is to "give something up," to deprive oneself of something enjoyable or habitual as a reminder of the sufferings of Jesus. Giving up pleasures such as candy, ice cream, alcohol, tobacco, coffee, etc., are popular. A modern Catholic should consider giving up activities even more habit-forming than food and drink. Some Catholics will give up use of their mobile phones (gasp!) for at least part of each day. Others will limit their use of the Internet and social media (really tough). Yet other Catholics will do something positive, not just give up something, for a Lenten observance. You could spend a specific period daily in spiritual reading or make a point to be nice to an unpleasant neighbor.

14. Attend a Lenten Fish-Fry

The No-Meat-on-Fridays-in-Lent rule creates the opportunity for Catholic schools and parishes to stage fundraisers by selling seafood on Friday nights during Lent. Lots of Catholics will be going out to eat seafood on those nights, so get them to the school cafeteria or parish hall and sell them a meal that agrees with the church rule. The parish Men's Club and other organizations provide the cooks, the servers, and the cleaners. The event provides for socialization and fellowship among members of the parish and others, including non-Catholics who simply like fried seafood. The ready availability of inexpensive and tasty farm-raised catfish allows fish-fry planners to charge a rate that is affordable to almost everyone. Some fish-fry events get fancier (and more expensive) by adding shrimp and oysters and crab cakes. By attending a fish-fry, Catholics can do more to support their parish than dropping a few bucks in the collection basket.

The parish fish-fry also is an escape from observing the Lenten rule at home with canned tuna fish (yuck!) or fish sticks (gasp!) or vegetarian pizza (so dull) or similar less-than-appetizing fare. Of course, Catholics with a culinary flair could choose to dine on swordfish steak, crawfish étouffée, and softshell crab. Even turtle, frog legs, and alligator are considered not to be meat for the purposes of the Lenten rule, which thus allows Catholics to enjoy Fridays even as they observe the penitential rite. Abstaining from hot dogs and potted meat is more fun when it can be done with a meal of lobster thermidor or oysters Rockefeller.

There's no church rule that says that Lent, like medicine of old, has to taste bad.

15. Contribute to Lenten Rice Bowls

An important devotion, integral to the observance of Lent, is giving alms, supporting the poor and the hungry of the world. Every Lent, the Catholic Relief Services (CRS) sponsors a program to encourage performing this activity. Parishes and schools order small cardboard rice-bowl boxes from CRS for distribution to individuals who participate. The boxes are used to deposit loose change and other contributions. Some Catholic schools pass them out to their students to teach them about Lent and the importance of charity. The children, as well as adults, are encouraged to make regular contributions during Lent into their rice bowls. The funds are collected by CRS and used to support their mission in parts of the United States and overseas where people do not have enough to eat, hence the name Rice Bowl. Twenty-five percent of CRS's Rice Bowl collections are used to alleviate hunger and poverty in American parishes. The remainder is used in ninety-three different countries. In addition to outright supplying of food, the funds are used to help poor farmers increase production, to assist in local medical services, and to finance the delivery of clean water.

The cardboard box is accompanied by a calendar with daily reflections and prayer, also vital parts of Lenten devotion.

The program was started decades ago when loose change was part of daily life and had greater buying power. The Rice Bowl program now includes an app that can be downloaded onto one's phone, and contributions can be made by the touch of a finger rather than digging into pockets and poking around in cabinet drawers for spare change. Catholics without the cardboard box or the app on their phones can send a check to CRS. There are many ways to conduct Lenten almsgiving.

16. Assist in the R.C.I.A.

Quick. What does R.C.I.A. stand for? Just as hardly anybody remembers that ATM stands for "Automated Teller Machine," most Catholics do not remember or ever knew that R.C.I.A. is the mouthful designation in ecclesiastical bureaucratese for "Rite of Christian Initiation of Adults." This is the process of instruction, study, prayer, and reflection through which an adult becomes a Catholic. Most parishes have programs established for welcoming new members to the Church and preparing them for Baptism or, if already baptized, for full participation in the life of the Catholic Church.

Depending on local practice, the process can take many months or more. Often the final steps are achieved during Lent. The practice goes back to the earliest days of the Church, when the Christian community instructed potential newcomers in their beliefs and devotions. Modern practice replicates that early Church experience, calling those in preparation "Catachumens." Typically, the Catachumens will attend the first part of the Sunday Mass, through the reading of the Gospel for that day. They will then be blessed by the priest and sent with their instructors for prayer and study in the tenets of Christianity and Catholicism. There is much to learn about a religion that has been an active force in world civilization for 2,000 years; there is much theology to learn about Jesus, the sacraments, the saints, and devotions.

Contemporary society becomes more and more secularized. People can reach adulthood without knowing what holidays such as Christmas and Easter stand for, let alone understand the meaning of those celebrations. The R.C.I.A. provides the opportunity for Catholics to share their knowledge and love of the Faith with others who are inquiring and want to join the club. Besides, in preparing to teach the Catachumens, a Catholic can increase his or her own knowledge and deepen devotion. Add to your bucket list to assist someone in the R.C.I.A.

17. Read the Bible

Catholics have been accused by other Christians of not reading or actually being prohibited from reading the Holy Scriptures. Lent is a good time to respond to that charge, which may have some superficial truth in it. Because the focus in Catholic worship is the Mass, the Bible seems secondary. But at every Mass there are readings from the Bible, mostly the New Testament. Reading the Bible opens up the ancient texts to a new appreciation for the stories and lessons in its many books.

The stories of Adam and Eve and the serpent and of Noah and the flood and the rainbow are part of the larger culture, tossed around by people who are only vaguely aware of their origins, let alone the deeper meanings. Reading in the Old Testament the vaguely remembered stories of Queen Esther, Rachel and the lost children, King Solomon, David and Goliath, Samson and Delilah, and Joshua and the Battle of Jericho provides an appreciation for their historical, theological, and literary importance.

Everybody knows the story of Moses leading the Hebrews out of captivity in Egypt and parting the Red Sea so that they could escape into the Sinai wilderness. But what are the events leading up to that dramatic passage and what happened after they escaped? Who was Joseph and why did he have a coat of many colors? Why was Daniel tossed into a den of lions? What happened? Being able to discuss these biblical stories can give Catholics a better understanding of the depths of their religion and what the references to older scriptures in the Gospels meant to the teaching of Jesus.

The same is true for the Old Testament prophets, especially Isaiah, who foretold the coming of Jesus as Messiah. For a real challenge, read some of the minor prophets such as Joel, Micah, Amos, Hosea, Malachi. Generations ago, Bible-focused Protestants named their children after some of these Old Testament figures. Is anyone naming children Ezekiel, Nahum, Bathsheba, and Tamar recently? There are lots of names to choose from in both the Old and the New Testaments.

18. Revel in the History of St. Patrick's Day

Not Irish? Not Catholic? On St. Patrick's Day it doesn't matter. Everybody is Irish on March 17 and thus Catholic by affinity, osmosis, and propinquity. All things green, shamrocks, and leprechauns have come to symbolize, especially to Americans, Ireland, Irish heritage, and an excuse to have a parade and a party in late winter.

What often gets lost in the gaiety is the fact that Patrick is a canonized saint of the Catholic Church, a holy man credited with converting the pagan Irish to Christianity in the fifth century. Despite Patrick's association with all things Irish, he was not Irish. He was a Christian in Roman Britain and was kidnapped by

Irish pirates when he was a young teenager. After several years he escaped, returned to Britain, and felt a call from God to convert his captors to Christianity. He sailed back to Ireland, and his efforts to bring the Catholic faith to the pagans were successful beyond anyone's imagination. Ireland became one of the most intensely Catholic countries in the world. Monasteries were established on remote, craggy islands as defense from Viking raiders. Learning flourished in those monasteries, and it was the monks living in them who kept Western Civilization alive when Europe descended into the Dark Ages and centers of knowledge were destroyed by Barbarians, Vikings, and roaming bands of thugs.

Perhaps St. Patrick should be toasted on his feast day (with Irish beer or Irish whisky, of course) for indirectly saving Western Civilization from destruction. Had the Irish monks not been inspired by Patrick's holiness and intensity, the monasteries would never have existed. Remember the legend of the snakes and Patrick? Today, maybe St. Patrick can help Florida do something about all those pythons that are ruining the Everglades.

St. Patrick's Day is a time when Catholics can revel in their history and trace their ancestors, actual or figurative, to the Emerald Isle.

19. Celebrate St. Joseph's Day

March 19 is usually in the middle of Lent. It is the important Feast of St. Joseph, husband of Mary, foster father to Jesus. In the nineteenth century, St. Joseph became an especially popular saint in southern Italy and particularly in Sicily. The tradition is that through prayers to St. Joseph, a famine was relieved, saving many from starvation. The faithful promised to thank the saint in perpetuity, and ever since, Sicilians and their descendants throughout the world have staged public parades and feasts to continue Joseph's blessing on their ancestors.

Sicilian-Americans in several cities where their forebears had

settled observe the day with offerings of food specially prepared for the occasion. Coming as it does in Lent, the proliferation of food is in contrast to the fasting and abstinence associated with Lent. But there is no meat at a St. Joseph's Day altar or dinner. And most of the food prepared for the feast is, following a blessing by a priest, distributed to those in need. Tasting the food and sipping some good Sicilian red wine will convince anyone that God is indeed good. Maybe he's Sicilian too.

Not just Sicilian-Americans celebrate St. Joseph Day. Polish and Polish-American Catholics honor the saint and all those named for him by wearing red and spreading a fine table in his honor. Anyone, whether Catholic or not, Sicilian or Polish or not, who finds himself or herself on March 19 in a city with a history of immigrants celebrating St. Joseph's Day should check out the local festivities. There are observances and celebrations in New York City, Buffalo, and Syracuse, New York; Hoboken, New Jersey; New Orleans, Louisiana; and Chicago, Illinois. Just as everyone is Irish on St. Patrick's Day, everyone can be Italian or Sicilian or Polish on St. Joseph's Day.

20. Pray the Stations of the Cross

The Way of the Cross, also called "doing the stations," is an old devotion that seems to have been deemphasized after the Second Vatican Council. It is often performed as a Lenten devotion in groups, typically on Fridays in Lent. At each of the fourteen stations, the faithful meditate on steps taken in Jesus' painful journey from condemnation by Pontius Pilate to being buried in the tomb from which he will rise on Easter. Pope John Paul II added a fifteenth station, the Resurrection, to show that the Way of the Cross ends in triumph.

One of the reasons for the downplay of the practice is that

JESUS FALLS FOR THE THIRD TIME.
TERECIRA CAIDA DE JESUS.

some of the events memorialized in the figurative, devotional journey are not based on scripture. For example, at the sixth station a woman named Veronica wipes Jesus' face, covered with sweat and blood. The legend is that his image was permanently imprinted on Veronica's veil, inspiring many entrepreneurs in the Middle Ages to entice the faithful to view and touch Veronica's veil—for a price, of course. The name "Veronica" is an amalgam of two Greek words meaning "true image." The three separate falls of Jesus along the Way of the Cross, stations three, seven, and nine, are not in any Gospel either.

Nevertheless, praying the Way of the Cross during Lent is a way for Catholics to feel a more personal closeness with Jesus, understanding his anxiety, his pain, his suffering, his anguish. Often, between each station, the faithful will chant a verse from the haunting Gregorian hymn, the *"Stabat Mater,"* the first verse of which is as follows:

Stabat Mater Dolorosa   The sorrowful mother was standing
Iuxta crucem, lachrymosa,   near the cross, crying,
Dum pendebat Filus.   while her son was hanging there.

Stark. Dark. Deeply moving.

21. Reenact Palm Sunday

This day could have just as easily been called "Cloak Sunday." All four Gospels write of Jesus' triumphal entry into Jerusalem and how the enthusiastic residents spread their cloaks before him. For this special, last journey into the holy city, Jesus was riding on a donkey. The donkey, sometimes translated as "ass," is a symbol of humility. The cheering crowd also greeted Jesus with branches, some of which may have been fronds from palm trees. It was a joyous occasion, but the enthusiasm of the greeters made some of the local Jerusalem fat cats uneasy. They didn't like the idea of a charismatic holy man from out of town encroaching on their turf.

Today Catholics—and other Christians too—observe the Sunday before Easter as the day Jesus was greeted with waved branches and palm fronds and cloaks spread on the road when he arrived in the city where he would soon be condemned to death. Every Catholic should participate in the procession into church on Palm Sunday, a reenactment of the events in Jerusalem. No donkeys or cloaks in the road are necessary for this devotion, but carrying and waving the palm branches are an excellent way to get in the mood of the day.

Weather permitting, the ritual starts outside the church with a blessing of the palms or other branches, which are then distributed to the congregation. Then all form a procession into the church singing or chanting music for the occasion. Depending on local practice (and whether the pastor is tuned into the musical phenomenon of the early 1970s), the congregation and choir could sing "Hosanna, Hey-Sanna" from *Jesus Christ Superstar*.

Palm Sunday begins the most solemn period in the church calendar, Holy Week. It will conclude the following Sunday, Easter.

22. Observe Holy Thursday

Lent comes to an end on Holy Thursday. When the liturgy begins on the evening of the Thursday after Palm Sunday, it marks the official end of Lent and the beginning of three holy days leading up to the celebration of the Resurrection of Jesus. The period is called the Easter Triduum or the Paschal Triduum, using an old word for Easter. Catholics observe the sacred time by attending the special—and long—services on those three days.

Don't wait for Easter Sunday. There is much rich tradition in observing Holy Thursday, the commemoration of the Last Supper and Jesus' creation of the Holy Eucharist. The scriptural readings at Mass begin with the story of the Passover, when the Hebrews were in slavery in Egypt. At the Last Supper Jesus and his disciples, devout Jews all, were observing this solemn Jewish holy day. Jesus knew it would be his last, and he used the occasion to give his "new commandment" to his followers: "Love one another as I have loved you." He also gave them the Holy Eucharist, saying as he blessed the bread, "This is my body."

During the first part of Mass, there is triumphal music and lots of bells. Then the mood becomes more solemn, as it did at the

National Gallery of Art, Washington, Gallery Archives

Last Supper with Jesus anxious about what could happen to him. Emulating the act of humility Jesus performed that night, the celebrant ritually washes the feet of twelve laypeople chosen for the occasion. Although not every Catholic can be among those who get their feet washed, participating in the service is just as devotional.

At the conclusion of the Mass of the Lord's Supper, the main altar is stripped bare, and there is a procession inside the church to take the consecrated bread to a repository for distribution the next day, Good Friday. During the march, the Gregorian hymn *"Pange Lingua"* ("Sing, My Tongue") is chanted. The service ends with dramatic silence and near darkness to set the mood for Good Friday.

23. Attend the Good Friday Liturgy

The most solemn day on the Catholic calendar is officially called Good Friday of the Lord's Passion. That is because the focus of the liturgy that day is the reading of the section of St. John's Gospel that details the suffering, the condemnation, the journey from one official to another until Pontius Pilate issues a death decree, and the crucifixion and death of Jesus. There is no Mass on Good Friday, and the communion wafers distributed at the service were consecrated during the Holy Thursday Mass the evening before.

Every Catholic should attend the Good Friday liturgy at least once. The ceremony lasts longer than regular Sunday Mass, but the solemnity of the occasion and the meaning of the death of Jesus make the day very special. The liturgy is usually scheduled at 3:00 P.M., the traditional time of Jesus' death after hanging on the cross for three hours. Thirteen states have made Good Friday a public holiday, and many large institutions, such as the New York Stock Exchange, observe the day as a break from regular business.

If attendance at the Good Friday liturgy is not possible, a Catholic can use the occasion to perform the Stations of the Cross, as discussed earlier. Many church parishes will schedule the Way of the Cross devotion at least once on Good Friday, in addition to the special liturgy.

Good Friday is the one other day besides Ash Wednesday that Catholics are required by church regulation to fast and to abstain from meat.

24. Celebrate Easter Vigil Mass

The most important event in the liturgical year begins with a ceremony that could make the fire marshal say prayers to St. Florian, patron of firefighters.

On Saturday night before Easter, the service begins with the church dark, lights out. The darkness symbolizes the inside of the tomb where Jesus was buried on Good Friday. As the congregation enters, each person is given an unlighted candle. At the rear of the church, or just outside, a fire is started. Called the "New Fire," it is a symbol of Christ as light of the world, rising from the dead. As hymns are chanted, the ministers light candles from the New Fire and spread the fire around the church to the members of the congregation, all of whom are holding their candles. When all candles are on fire, the church is full of light—and some smoke too. Christ has overcome the darkness through his Resurrection.

In preparation for attending the Easter Vigil service, be sure to visit the bathroom beforehand. The Easter Vigil is long and dramatic, with lots of music and burning of incense. The large Paschal candle is ceremoniously blessed and lighted, and there are many readings from scripture. Some churches, cathedrals, and monasteries use the full, long form of the Easter Vigil, which spreads the service out over several hours.

The full service is moving and dramatic, and it is no longer than a feature movie and shorter than grand opera. Attending the Easter Vigil leaves one with a rich and deep sense of the meaning and importance of the Resurrection. And everyone gets to take the candle home.

Although clearly out of the budgetary reach of most Catholics, it would be really exciting to celebrate Easter Mass on Easter Island as the sun rises in the Pacific Ocean.

25. Participate in a Baptism

You're not a Catholic unless you're baptized. Most Catholics are baptized as infants, but those who join the church as adults are also baptized. Baptism is an integral part of the Easter Vigil service, if there are persons to be baptized. Catholics who are already baptized can participate in this ceremony, initiating new members into the Catholic Church. In addition to the parents of the baptized child, there are godparents who participate. For the Baptism of adults, there are sponsors in lieu of godparents. The Baptism of adults at the Easter Vigil is the culmination of the R.C.I.A. process. (Do you remember what those initials stand for?)

Baptism is full of symbolism. The ceremony recalls how John the Baptist baptized Jesus in the Jordan River. Water implies that sin is washed away. The newly baptized person receives a blessed candle and a white cloth as signs of their becoming members of the Church. The candle is lighted from the large Easter candle and is a reminder that Christ is the light of the world. The white cloth or the white Christening gown shows that sin has been washed away.

Baptism also includes an anointing of the baptized with Holy Chrism, oil mixed with balsam, an ancient symbol going back to the Old Testament and the Psalms. Anointing means the person is special and blessed by God.

Although in most Catholic churches Baptism is performed by pouring a small amount of water on the head, some churches practice adult Baptism by immersion, completely sinking the person into a tub of water, just as is done in many Protestant churches. Whether the water is just a trickle across the head or a complete immersion, the validity of the sacrament is the same. As a just-baptized person is shaking the holy water out of his hair and rubbing his eyes, this may be a good time to greet the new Catholic with "Welcome to the Catholic Church!"

Parent, godparent, sponsor, friend—there are several ways to participate in the sacrament.

26. Study Up on Confirmation

Confirmation is complementary to the sacrament of Baptism. Most Catholics are baptized as infants or children and have no decision-making power. Confirmation is usually a coming-of-age event, when an adolescent can decide to affirm the effects of Baptism. If adults are baptized at the Easter Vigil service, they can be confirmed immediately after Baptism. The sacrament of Confirmation is usually administered by a bishop. He lays his hands on the person being confirmed and, just as was done at Baptism, anoints the person with Holy Chrism. Once again, the holy oil symbolizes that an important theological event has taken place, the invocation of the Holy Spirit. The bishop concludes the ritual with a slight slap to the cheek of the confirmed. This is a reminder that every Christian must be prepared to endure, as Shakespeare might say, the slings and arrows of rebuke and persecution done because of one's Faith.

Adult Catholics who have never been confirmed should study up on the importance of the sacrament. Every culture seems to have a rite of passage from childhood to adulthood. Graduation from high school is a secular rite of passage. In Judaism, the Bat Mitzvah and Bar Mitzvah are celebrated. Confirmation is how a Catholic progresses from an adolescent understanding of the Faith to a mature one.

An infant does not get to choose a name for Baptism. The child is baptized invoking a saint's name that is to be patron for life. But at Confirmation you get to pick your own saint. This can be an interesting process if you study the history of that saint. Choose some obscure saint such as St. Ethelreda or St. Pancras. As the bishop confirms you under the chosen saint's name, he'll be wondering where in the world you found that saint.

27. Go to Confession, the Sacrament of Reconciliation

When's the last time you went to confession? Remember kneeling in the dark booth and beginning "Bless me, Father, for I have sinned"? Churches used to have long lines outside the confessional booths. Pious Catholics would seek to make amends for sins ranging from eating meat on Friday to marital infidelity to harboring "evil thoughts" such as wishing harm on someone or sexual fantasies involving someone else's spouse. Many Catholics thought that going to confession was a prerequisite to receiving Holy Communion.

Changes came. The Sacrament of Penance had its name changed to the Sacrament of Reconciliation, better to reflect the theology of the relationship between penitent and God. Then the notion of sin itself sort of dissipated, and the lines on Saturday afternoon inside churches grew shorter and shorter.

But wait. Sin is still around, at least as much as it's always been. The theological notion of sin is irrelevant or nonexistent to a deeply secularized culture. Believers know that their friendship with God is often marred by disorderly and even shameful acts and omissions, essentially treating a parent or friend in a way that damages the love and the connection. This is where Reconciliation comes in to heal the rifts. You want to stay friends with God? This sacrament is a big help.

28. Receive the Eucharist or Holy Communion

A child's First Communion is a big deal, and well it should be. The Eucharist is probably the most important of the seven sacraments in that it celebrates the reception of the body and blood of Jesus by the communicant. The Eucharist replicates Jesus' actions at the Last Supper when he broke bread with his disciples, shared it with them, and announced that the bread was his body. The sacrament is mystical and defies ordinary reason, but that's what makes it so important; it is above and beyond reason.

A second-grade child making First Communion is not going to understand the mystical significance of the sacrament, but family and friends make the event a celebration that the child will remember for life, understanding that something really important happened that gave a connection to Jesus Christ.

Catholic family and friends participate not only by attending the Mass and the ceremony but also by offering congratulations and gifts. This is the occasion for the godparents who participated in the child's Baptism a few years earlier to continue to encourage the child's Faith by providing prayer books, a rosary, a "holy picture" or two, a crucifix for the bedroom, and many other items that a local Catholic bookstore will be happy to sell to you.

After your First Communion, you begin a lifetime of Holy Communions, the tenth and the nine-hundredth and the ten-thousandth. This is the ultimate intimacy with God, consuming the body and blood of Jesus.

THE HOLY EUCHARIST
LA SAGRADA EUCARISTÍA.

29. Attend an Ordination

Getting ordained can't be on every Catholic's life list. To begin with, fewer than half the Catholics on earth are eligible. Someday women may be allowed to become deacons and priests, but currently only men can be ordained. But a Catholic should attend an ordination at least once. It is a very solemn ceremony that begins with the men to be ordained lying face down on the floor of the church for quite a while as a gesture of humility and submission to God. The bishop sits in a large chair overlooking the prostrate men, grasping his crozier (staff of his office) in such a grip that onlookers begin to wonder whether his excellency is going to pummel the men who lie in a position of vulnerability before him. This would not be a way to encourage more vocations to the diaconate or the priesthood.

Catholics can be indirect participants in Holy Orders even if they cannot attend an ordination or otherwise be part of the ritual. There is often talk of a shortage of priests, and there are prayers at Mass for men to answer the call to become one. In addition, most dioceses have chapters of a network called Serra International, an organization of Catholic men and women who actively work to encourage men to enter the priesthood and support those who are considering it. Not to be confused with the conservationist group the Sierra Club, Serra International is nevertheless named for another feature of California history and geography, St. Junipero Serra, the Franciscan friar who established missions along the Pacific coast in the eighteenth century.

The decision to become a priest is not made lightly, and men considering priestly service as their life's vocation need encouragement and support. Serra International is organized to do that. And once the man gets through the rigors of preparation, the support group can be there to witness his ordination and receipt of Holy Orders.

30. Receive the Sacrament of Matrimony

Getting married in the Catholic Church is a big deal, as well it should be. Matrimony is a sacrament, an event created by Jesus Christ to bring grace and dignity to the couple. The popularity of cohabitation without marriage is undeniable, but the couple in such a relationship misses out on the blessing of God and the Church that will enhance their connection of love and make it durable.

The theological basis of Matrimony is interesting. Although a priest or a deacon will administer the sacrament as a function of church law, he does not confer the sacrament on the couple; they confer it on themselves, and the minister is there to make it official. The couple and God are the essential participants. The ceremony can be very simple, with the couple exchanging vows before a few witnesses, or it can be very elaborate—and expensive—with a big, blowout wedding in a cathedral with a choir and hundreds of guests attending the nuptial mass and waiting to get to the reception for free food and beverages. (Think *My Big Fat Catholic Wedding.*)

So important is Matrimony that Jesus chose a wedding for the site of his first public miracle, turning vats of water into wine. If the custom in Galilee 2,000 years ago was as today, that the bride's family picks up the tab for the wedding reception, then the father of the bride was about to be very embarrassed when the chief steward announced (one would hope not to the assembled guests) that they had run out of wine. At this point Mother Mary told her son to do something about the empty wine jars. Although at first reluctant, Jesus honored his mother's request, and more wine appeared in jars that had been filled with water. The event was that important.

Rock-'n'-roller Jerry Lee Lewis (not a Catholic) was asked on the occasion of his fifth or sixth marriage why he didn't just live with the woman. "I don't want to be living in sin," said the flamboyant musician. If nothing else, Matrimony is avoiding living in sin.

But it is a lot more.

31. Celebrate May Crowning

Springtime! Flowers! Children in procession! Few celebrations are as distinctly Catholic as the May crowning of Mary as "Queen of the May." Usually done outdoors, where a procession can wind through the church grounds to a statue of Mary, the ceremony may be kept inside the church by weather. This is a celebration of the unique position of Mary in Catholicism.

In the nineteenth century, the pope dedicated the month of May to Mary. There are many "Mary" days in the month: the Saturday following Ascension Day is the Feast of Mary, Queen of the Apostles; Our Lady of the Blessed Sacrament and Our Lady of Fatima are celebrated on May 13; on May 24 is the Feast of Mary, Help of Christians, and Mary, Mediatrix of All Graces; and May 31 is the Feast of the Visitation, the event when Mary visited her cousin Elizabeth and both announced they were pregnant, Mary with Jesus, Elizabeth with John the Baptist.

Children carry flowers, in procession with adults, while singing hymns to Mary. Children's voices on a fine spring morning uplift participants' spirits, and adults will feel nostalgia and a connection to the Catholicism of their past, remembering that they too were once the children in the May crowning procession. Can you remember?

> O, Mary, we crown you with flowers today,
> Queen of the angels, Queen of the May.

If the May crowning procession is held inside the church, there is nothing more inspiring than a fine Irish tenor with a rich voice pouring out his soul and devotion as the spring sun beams in through the stained-glass windows. It is a time to remember the verse of Robert Browning from "Pippa Passes":

> The year's at the Spring
> And day's at the morn;
> Morning's at seven,
> The hillside's dew-pearled,
> The lark's on the wing;
> The snail's on the thorn.
> God's in His heaven—
> All's right with the world.

32. Attend Mass on Ascension Day

According to the Gospels of Mark and Luke and the Book of Acts, Jesus, in the presence of some of his disciples, left the earth for heaven forty days after Easter. This event became known as "Ascension Thursday" and is a holy day of obligation that slips by a lot of Catholics. As with some other holy days, the bishops of the United States understood that getting to church for Mass on a school and work day was enough of a burden to make a lot of otherwise pious Catholics forget the feast day and miss Mass.

The bishops are a practical bunch (some of them, some of the time) and so they simply shifted the observance of the feast day to the nearest Sunday, although some dioceses still observe the traditional Thursday. By placing the Ascension on Sunday, more Catholics will likely attend Mass and share in the theological

National Gallery of Art, Washington, Gallery Archives

importance of the event. The Sunday schedule means they also can avoid the sense of guilt in missing Mass on a holy day of obligation. After his Resurrection, Jesus made many appearances. He wasn't immediately recognized by his followers. This is understandable. The last time they had seen him he was bloody, beaten, hanging on a cross, dead. Here he was days later in what is called a "glorified" body, an existence that is outside the usual restrictions of physics and biology. These apparitions, and especially the Ascension, were to show his followers that he was indeed God and had come back from the tomb. In the act of the Ascension, Jesus is also inviting believers to follow him to union in heaven.

Catholics should always make the effort to attend Mass on this important feast day, whether it occurs on Thursday or Sunday.

33. Chant "Come, Holy Ghost" on Pentecost

Fifty days after Easter, Jesus' disciples were cowering, hiding out because they were afraid that they too would be arrested and punished, even crucified, just like what happened to their leader. The Book of Acts describes what happened next: the Holy Spirit came down on them "like tongues of fire" and instilled in them the resolve to do what they had been chosen to do, create the Church of Jesus Christ by going out into the world and preaching his message of love and reconciliation.

Pentecost gets its name from the Greek word for "fifty." Were there Greek speakers among the disciples gathered that day?

National Gallery of Art, Washington, Gallery Archives

Who knows? The point is that the inspiration of the Holy Spirit gave them the courage and the energy to shed their fears and reluctance and speak to the world in many languages. Pentecost is considered to be the birthday of the Christian Church. There was no birthday cake in the room where the disciples were hiding out, but there was fire. The image of fire is appropriate because the Holy Spirit sent not only fire upon them but put fire into their bellies to get them off their duffs. In some churches the Pentecost fire of the Holy Spirit is displayed on statues of some of the apostles as a flame on the top of their heads.

The fire inspires the color of the vestments worn by priests and deacons on Pentecost, bright red. It is the color used in other liturgies in honor of the Holy Spirit, including the sacrament of Confirmation.

Pentecost provides the opportunity to chant and listen to one of the great Gregorian hymns, *"Veni Creator Spiritus,"* and the English hymn "Come, Holy Ghost." It also is an occasion to explain to children and others confused by the use of the word that the Holy Ghost has nothing to do with Halloween. The Holy Ghost had a name change to Holy Spirit, to make the English translation of *Spiritus Sanctus* more up to date.

34. Support the Canopy on the Feast of Corpus Christi

Corpus Christi is not just a city in Texas. It is a feast day established in the thirteenth century as a way to honor and adore the Eucharist in public, not just inside the church building. The full Latin name of the holy day is *Corpus et Sanguis Christi* ("The Body and Blood of Christ"). It is observed on the Thursday following Trinity Sunday, which is the Sunday following Pentecost. In the United States it is usually observed on the Sunday after Trinity Sunday, by the English name of the feast day.

The celebration involves carrying the consecrated host in a solemn procession into the streets, or at least outside the church. After Mass, a consecrated host is placed in a monstrance. That's a receptacle made for the display of the consecrated Eucharist, with a glass-covered container surrounded by ornamental devices, usually gold, that suggest rays of light coming from the center. As the procession begins after Mass, the congregation joins in the march and in the singing of hymns. The traditional hymns honoring the Eucharist were composed in Latin and chanted in Gregorian style, such as *"O Salutaris Hostia"* and *"Pange Lingua,"* but they have been translated into English, or suitable English hymns are substituted.

The procession is an opportunity for Catholics to participate in a seldom-performed ritual, the carrying of the canopy that covers the priest as he walks holding the monstrance. The canopy is supported by four staffs to keep it above the priest. It has the arcane name of *baldachin,* which sounds as though someone has just shaved a beard off his face. With or without a beard, carrying the baldachin is an opportunity for Catholics to get closer to God.

35. Participate in Benediction

Every Catholic should occasionally participate in the devotion of Benediction. Like the procession on the Feast of Corpus Christi, Benediction is a way of expressing particular homage to the consecrated Eucharist. This belief in the "real presence," that Jesus Christ is truly present in the bread and wine consecrated at Mass, is one of the identifying markers of Catholicism that distinguishes it from many other Christian religions.

Benediction is often held after some other devotion such as the Stations of the Cross, a novena, or a spiritual retreat. The deacon or priest wears a special shawl around his shoulders while holding the vessel used for devotion. The shawl is called a "humeral veil" because it is worn around the shoulders. The deacon or priest removes the consecrated bread from the tabernacle and places it in the monstrance, the ceremonial vessel described previously in the section on Corpus Christi. If a monstrance is not used, the consecrated host is kept in the ciborium, a chalice-like bowl in which the consecrated bread is stored in the tabernacle.

The hymns sung during Benediction are the same as those at Corpus Christi, "*O Salutaris Hostia*" and "*Tantum Ergo.*" English-language hymns are often substituted so that the congregation can sing along and participate fully.

Benediction is usually accompanied by burning incense, which smolders in a device called a "thurible" or "censer." An acolyte swings the thurible at the end of a three-chain harness to cause a breeze to make the incense burn better. The smoke and aroma of incense imprint in memory an image that is instantly and firmly "Catholic." Catholicism has been identified humorously as the religion of "bells and smells." Benediction incense is the second part of that identity. Sniff a whiff and feel Catholic.

36. Make a Retreat

In the lyrics to the "Battle Hymn of the Republic," Julia Ward Howe wrote, "He has sounded forth the trumpet that shall never call retreat." Those words invoke a warlike God with a "terrible swift sword," not the compassionate and forgiving Jesus of the New Testament. Catholics *should* call retreat, retreat from the pressures of daily living for a few days of prayer, spiritual reading, reflection. After all, Jesus made a retreat of forty days before beginning his public life. His example shows that a spiritual retreat is something that ought to be done before someone embarks on an important part of his life. St. Ignatius of Loyola, founder of the Society of Jesus, the Jesuits, composed the Spiritual Exercises that every Jesuit must perform before becoming a full-fledged member of the order. The Exercises are a thirty-day retreat done in silence and with the guidance of a retreat master.

St. Ignatius's Exercises have been modified so that laymen, few of whom live lives that permit them to drop out for thirty days, can experience the uplift and cleansing that the Exercises provide. Thus this form of retreat is available to most Catholics. As one proceeds through the Exercises and feels the results of Ignatius's method of discernment, the mind and heart are opened to a fresh experience with the closeness of God.

Retreats can be done in other ways too. Some retreat centers include opportunities for group discussions and shared reflections, not just silent contemplation. The point is that a retreat is a visit to a spiritual spa where a Catholic can get a theological massage and perform soul-stretching exercises to release the cramps of daily life and become loose and limber in prayer life.

37. Make a Day of Recollection

Don't have time or opportunity to make a full retreat? A Day of Recollection is an abbreviated version of a multiday retreat, such as the Spiritual Exercises of St. Ignatius of Loyola. Many parishes and retreat centers offer various types of days of recollection, from full silence to full vocal participation. Some days have themes, such as devotion to Mary or to the Sacred Heart of Jesus or to one of the saints. The point is there are multiple ways of getting closer to God.

Like a retreat, a Day of Recollection usually has a leader or facilitator of the event, helping guide the participants through a day of prayer, reflection, and meditation. The focus may be on a particular section or passage in the Bible, the practice of the Corporal Works of Mercy (more about them later), the various themes ("mysteries") of the rosary, or the life of a particular saint who may be especially inspiring.

Although a Day of Recollection is more effective spiritually when done with a group and a director or leader, a Catholic can make a personal, impromptu day. It's not necessary to sit all day inside a dark church, but if that inspires, so be it. A visit to the grounds of a convent or monastery might reveal a shrine or other outdoor setting fit for meditation. Saying the rosary and walking the Stations of the Cross can also be done individually, as well as with a group.

As with all prayerful activities, a Day of Recollection helps bring someone closer to God.

38. Make a General Confession

A retreat, Day of Recollection, or Lent are the opportunities for receiving the Sacrament of Reconciliation in what is called a General Confession. Think of a General Confession as a major housekeeping operation that clears out all the cobwebs and mites and dust bunnies and crud that have been building up for a long time. By comparison, regular confession is like routine, periodic housekeeping. The place looks good, it's clean, it's ready for use, but there are some corners and crevices that need more attention before the house is in top shape for the arrival of some important guest or event.

The routine Sacrament of Reconciliation is complete with a confession of serious ("mortal") sins that have not been presented to God in formal confession. The General Confession, which makes the penitent examine the conscience more deeply and takes more time with the priest hearing the confession, needs special scheduling. That is why the usual practice of going to confession a few minutes before Mass while others are waiting in line is not the time for a General Confession.

Listening to people cough up their sins and failures before God must be one of the most unpleasant requirements of being a priest. Sure, he has the satisfaction of preparing souls for improving their friendship with God, but hearing tales of violence and vice, with graphic and lurid details, can be upsetting. That's why a time should be set aside for the General Confession so that priest and penitent can prepare themselves psychologically and spiritually for washing the dirty laundry of the soul.

39. Make a Novena

Imagine a Presbyterian making a novena. You can't. A novena is a devotion that has "Catholic" written all over it.

A novena consists of nine days of prayer, Mass, and Eucharist. The notion of nine days of worship is actually pre-Christian. The ancient Romans had nine-day periods of mourning for the dead, and, like many other pagan practices, the Catholic Church changed the event into a Christian observance.

The purpose of the novena varies with the person making it or the local church sponsoring the services. In some parishes a novena is held once a week throughout the year, not just nine days in one year. A Catholic can attend for nine days in nine weeks and will have completed the novena. Many scheduled, formal parish novenas are on nine consecutive days and are dedicated to a particular saint or to the Blessed Virgin Mary. Novenas are often prayers of petition; the person making them wants divine help or a favor. Novenas of petition to Our Lady of

Photograph by Anne Renouf, courtesy of the Jubilee Museum, Columbus, Ohio

Perpetual Help and St. Jude are popular. St. Jude Thaddeus was one of the original twelve apostles. Because his name led people to confuse him with Judas Iscariot, devotion to him waned after the Middle Ages. But he was brought out of obscurity in the early twentieth century with special prayers to him as the "Saint of the Impossible" or "Patron of Lost Causes." When Catholics feel desperate and want help, a novena to St. Jude is often the devotion of choice.

Novenas to Our Lady of Perpetual Help, the Sacred Heart of Jesus, and other saints can be prayers of petition, of thanksgiving, of mourning. Just be sure that the novena is nine days to be the most effective.

Don't have time to make a nine-day novena? Then you can do a "Flying Novena," saying the prayers of the formal novena nine times in one day. God hears all prayers, no matter if they are offered nine times in one day, once daily in nine days, or once weekly in nine weeks.

40. Complete the Nine First Fridays

The important number nine is part of the devotion of the First Fridays. In the seventeenth century, French nun St. Margaret Mary Alacoque had visions that resulted in specific instructions from Jesus to make devotions to his Sacred Heart. Such devotions had been part of Catholicism for centuries, but St. Margaret Mary's visions and evangelizing made them widespread. In order to receive the special grace and blessings of the Sacred Heart, these requirements must be met:

1. Attendance at Mass and reception of Holy Communion on first Fridays of nine consecutive months. No breaks, no skipping.
2. The Mass and communion offered in honor of the Sacred Heart of Jesus, not some other devotion or prayer of petition.

The devotion should be done by all Catholics. The purpose of St. Margaret Mary's exhortations is to bring all Catholics to a closer devotion to Jesus in his mystical manifestation as the Sacred Heart. In exchange for completing the nine First Fridays, Jesus promises solace and redemption, sharing eternity with him.

The devotion has inspired the formation of religious orders dedicated to the Sacred Heart. The Society of the Sacred Heart is a religious order for women. These nuns spread the word of God and devotion to the Sacred Heart throughout the world in schools and missions and other ways of communicating their message of love and devotion. The Brothers of the Sacred Heart are an order of religious brothers with similar missions.

The amount of art depicting Jesus with a heart flaming with love for mankind is amazing. Who has not seen the paintings of Jesus intently staring at the viewer, with flowing auburn hair and an elegant white gown, upon which the flaming Sacred Heart burns? Some of the pictures are sentimental, some kitsch, some inspiring. Did Jesus really look like that? Probably not.

41. Observe the Five First Saturdays

First Saturdays follow First Fridays, another opportunity to express Catholic identity. The devotion of the five First Saturdays began at Fatima, Portugal, in 1916-17. The Blessed Mother appeared several times to three children there while World War I was raging and tearing Europe apart. Her message to them was to pray, pray often, pray fervently for peace.

In her final apparition she gave instructions to the oldest child, Lucia Dos Santos. These included the request for devotions on the first Saturday of five consecutive months. On those days Catholics should go to confession, now called the Sacrament of Reconciliation; receive Holy Communion at Mass; recite five decades of the rosary (more about the rosary later); and meditate for at least fifteen minutes on all fifteen mysteries of the rosary. In return is a promise from Our Lady that she will be present at the hour of the worshiper's death to ease the soul's entry into heaven.

Although the children's visions were understandably met with skepticism, in a few years the devotion to Our Lady of Fatima grew, as did the attributions of healing and other miracles to the intercession of the Blessed Mother who had appeared to the children. This practice of observing the five First Saturdays as a special devotion to Mary is closely tied to the regular praying of the rosary.

There will be more about Fatima in a subsequent entry. And the rosary.

42. Bless Your Home

The tradition of the "housewarming" party is a way to introduce your home to friends and relatives, having their presence "warm" the home with their friendship and love. It's also a good excuse for a party. Why not combine it with a ceremony that invokes God's blessing on the home and your future in it?

The Catholic Church has developed a specific ritual for blessing a home. It invokes the instructions Jesus gave to his disciples when he sent them out to preach and teach and heal the sick. In the Gospel of St. Luke, Jesus is quoted as telling them, when they entered a house during their journey, to greet everyone present with "Peace to this house." Guests coming to the housewarming party would do well to greet the hosts with that same wish, along with the usual "Congratulations on your place." Later in the same chapter of Luke's Gospel is the story of Martha welcoming Jesus into her home.

Check with the pastor of your parish and see if he or a deacon can schedule an appearance and conduct the brief ceremony at your housewarming party. Most priests, deacons too, appreciate an invitation to a party with good food and beverages, so there shouldn't be much difficulty in getting a cleric to your house and having him sprinkle the rooms with holy water. It is also an opportunity to express your Catholicism to friends and relatives in a joyful and intimate setting, not just at Sunday Mass or a wedding or a funeral.

43. Install Home Holy Water Founts

Holy water founts, bowls actually, are features at the entrances of most Catholic churches. Some are simple dishes on a stand where an entering Catholic dips a finger or two and makes the Sign of the Cross. Others are elaborate pieces of art, with life-size statues of saints holding a bowl. The purpose is to place oneself in the presence of God by a self-reminder of where you are and why you're there.

Similar, smaller founts were once common in Catholic homes, with devices attached to the frames of bedroom doors as well as at the front door. When you entered or left the house, the fount was a reminder to bless yourself as part of the daily routine. The bedroom founts also provided the opportunity and reminder to conduct the self-blessing upon arising and before going to sleep.

The devices hanging on the doorframes were often made to represent a miniature angel, with long hair, big wings, and a tiny bowl cradled in the angel's arms. Into that bowl went holy water that was obtained at the church from a tank blessed as part of the Easter Vigil service. Inevitably founts would spill, and holy water would fall onto the floor or carpet. If the family pet happened to be nearby and lapped up some of the fallen holy water, interesting theological questions would emanate from the mouths of children: "Sammy [the dog] just drank some holy water? Is that a sin or does that mean she will go to heaven?" (St. Thomas Aquinas never had to deal with such heavy theological inquiries.)

Continuing this custom of holy water in the home and making the Sign of the Cross after dipping fingers is another way to exercise Catholic identity. Just be careful the founts get cleaned regularly and aren't overfilled. And if the dog gets to lick up a spill, so be it. Animals get blessed too, as St. Francis of Assisi demonstrated.

44. Celebrate the Assumption of Mary

This holy day of obligation is easy to miss. August 15 is in the middle of one of the slowest, hottest months of the year. The children are not yet back in school. It's hot. The family vacation is over; the "dog days" of summer are upon us. It's hot. Everyone is awaiting the approach of fall. It's hot. In the middle of these doldrums, Catholics are called upon to attend Mass in honor of Our Lady to mark a very mystical event in her life.

Early in Catholicism, possibly from Apostolic times, there developed a doctrine that Mary, after she died, was "assumed" into heaven. That means that, although she did not appear in public after death as Jesus did, God nevertheless allowed her to enter heaven with soul *and* body. It is as though Mary, because of her position as the mother of Jesus, met final judgment shortly after death without having to wait for the end of time like the rest of us mortal humans. In the Nicene Creed we profess belief in the "resurrection of the body," but that event will not happen until final judgment when, as the old hymn and the Book of Revelation predict, the "Saints go marchin' in." Mary got there first, and that glorious event is what Catholics celebrate on August 15, when it's hot.

In the Eastern Orthodox churches, this mystical event is a very important holy day. They designate it "The Dormition of the Theotokos." "Dormition" means "falling asleep," although Orthodox Church theology is that Mary died and her body was then "assumed" into heaven, as the Western Church proclaims. The title of "Theotokos" means "God-bearer," because Mary bore Jesus and delivered him into the world.

Catholics should fight the heat and celebrate the Assumption as a reminder that Mary is special and that all who share the grace of God will join her on the Last Day of time.

45. Feed the Hungry

Catholicism likes to number things. In addition to the seven sacraments and the fourteen Stations of the Cross, for example, there are the seven Corporal Works of Mercy, pious acts that manifest a person's commitment to the beliefs and requirements of being Catholic.

The first is to feed the hungry. There are a surprisingly large number of people in the United States as well as throughout the world who do not get enough to eat. Beggars gather at street intersections to ply motorists who must stop for a traffic light. We read about children in inner cities and in rural communities who show up at school hungry because there wasn't sufficient food in their homes for breakfast. No child can learn malnourished. They fall further behind and continue the culture of poverty, hunger, and ignorance. Feeding them is not just a Christian duty; it will benefit society at large by keeping children healthy.

Contributing to Catholic social-service agencies that serve food to hungry people is an obvious way to perform this work of mercy, so go ahead and volunteer at an event or for an organization that is routinely involved in getting meals to poor people. The local soup kitchen and Meals on Wheels organization that delivers meals to elderly poor people usually need helpers. Catholic schools, social-service clubs, and parishes sponsor Thanksgiving basket drives that bring dinners to those who would otherwise not have a holiday feast.

In many urban areas, community gardens have become popular as an environmentally beneficial use of vacant land and as part of the "Eat Local" movement. The resulting produce could be contributed to the local food bank or soup kitchen, which would help not only the environment but be a means of experiencing a closer relationship with God.

46. Give Drink to the Thirsty

The second of the seven Corporal Works of Mercy is to give drink to the thirsty. That beggar at the intersection may interpret this requirement for Christian mercy as getting money to buy some liquor or "street" wine. Obviously, many panhandlers have drinking and mental problems, so a bottle of water or juice or energy drink is a much better donation. Many people carry bottles of water or sports drinks in their vehicles to pass out when a sad, haggard person holds up a cardboard sign near a traffic light.

The beggar at the intersection is a very local example of a thirsty person in need of water. The United Nations estimates that more than 780 million people in the world lack clean water. Without clean water to drink and to wash their dishes and pots, it is no wonder that so many of them suffer from chronic diseases and experience high mortality. When disasters such as hurricanes, floods, and earthquakes damage or destroy what little clean-water infrastructure exists in developing countries, the need, an immediate one, for clean water becomes acute.

Catholic Relief Services (CRS) is heavily involved in bringing clean water to poor people throughout the world. Obviously an ordinary concerned Catholic can hardly be expected to hop on an airplane and go help dig a well or lay pipes in some far-off thirsty place. But monetary contributions to organizations such as CRS that are bringing clean water to remote parts of the world are how the work gets done.

Young Catholics who are just reaching adulthood may find adventure as well as a work of mercy by joining a group sponsoring a clean-water project somewhere far away or even relatively close to home.

While hanging on the cross, Jesus said, "I thirst." Let's do something about it.

47. Clothe the Naked

There was a silly fad in the 1970s called "streaking." A person, almost always male, would run through a public place such as a stadium or a boulevard, nude except for running shoes. There was no purpose or meaning to the practice, sort of like a child who runs outside naked to embarrass the parents. In 2004 another naked fad started, this time organized. World Naked Bike Ride spread internationally, on which day groups of nudists would ride bicycles through urban areas to highlight a cause or protest an injustice. When watching these antics, some people may have wanted to give the naked people some clothing, for modesty if not for warmth. These streakers and naked riders are not, however, those of whom Jesus spoke when he said, "When I was naked, you gave me some clothes." *See Matthew* 25:35.

Jesus was giving his followers a lesson in charity. He told them that whatever Corporal Works of Mercy they do, they do it to him. Thus if somebody is in need of clothing, a Christian should give the poor person something to wear as though that person were Jesus himself.

The Gospels never speak directly of Jesus being naked. But when he reached the place of crucifixion, Golgotha or Calvary, the guards removed his clothes and threw dice to see who would get them. Many, many years later, art depicting the crucifixion would show Jesus hanging on the cross wearing only a loincloth around his hips. That piece of clothing was for modesty's sake; Jesus probably hung naked on the cross in humiliation until he died.

In providing clothing to people who have none, Catholics can understand the humiliation of poverty, being so poor that one cannot afford a decent pair of shoes or underwear without holes. In giving clothes to the poor, a Catholic symbolically gives clothes back to Jesus.

It's OK to pronounce "naked" as "nekkid."

48. Shelter the Homeless

These unfortunate fellow human beings make the rest of us uncomfortable. They are at intersections with their cardboard signs and under viaducts and overpasses with their makeshift shelters and old shopping carts. They live in squalor and fear, often with only a dog for a friend. Although some are homeless simply because they are poor, most have psychological problems and suffer from drug and alcohol dependency. They are dirty and smelly and ill-mannered. They are God's children, and they need our help and love.

Most urban centers have one or more shelters for the homeless. These centers rely in part on contributions from private citizens and volunteer workers. That means you. The homeless need shelter, sure, but that is just a beginning. Most need counseling, medical and dental care, clothes as well as a place to eat. Many shelters are run by Catholic social-service agencies who need the help of laymen who understand the mandate of Jesus.

People are homeless for a reason. Dealing with those reasons can be difficult: mental illness, mental deficiency, physical disability, domestic violence. Battered women, some with

children, have a home, but their home is a place of physical and psychological danger. They need a safe haven from violence. Homelessness often seems to be an intractable problem. Some homeless people are so traumatized and paranoid that they prefer the street to a shelter. They seem incapable of living in a structured environment and socializing with others. Nevertheless, they cannot be abandoned to their madness. They need us. They are us.

Get involved with a local organization that ministers to the homeless. While you deal with the negative emotions and even revulsion, know that you are doing what Jesus expects you to do.

49. Visit the Sick

Your sister calls to say that Uncle Charlie has been hospitalized. He'll be going home soon, she says, and he'll have a long recuperation after the surgery. He'll need someone to stop by, do some chores around the house, cheer him up. Aunt Jane, his wife, can do only so much and needs help.

You don't like Uncle Charlie. He comes over and talks too loud, drinks too much, makes inappropriate remarks about family members. You want to say that Uncle Charlie can go jump in the lake. Or worse.

This is where the Christian imperative to love, to help others, stares you in the face. This is the fifth of the Corporal Works of Mercy. You remember that Uncle Charlie is your mother's brother, and you know she would be pleased if you visited him while he was incapacitated. You want to please Mama. You remember that Jesus visited a lot of sick people and cared for them. Some of them were rude, obnoxious. There is the story of the ten lepers whom Jesus healed and sent off to the priests to show that they were cleansed. Nine of them went off without thanking Jesus; only one came back to express his gratitude. With this story from St. Luke's Gospel on your mind, you say a quick prayer to St. Roch or some other patron of sick people and go visit Uncle Charlie.

Maybe he'll be rude, maybe he'll be nice, maybe he'll be indifferent and ungrateful. But by visiting him you have shown him that you care, if not for him so much as for Jesus. And for your mama.

50. Visit the Imprisoned

Go directly to jail. Do not pass GO. Do not collect $200.

That command may be part of playing Monopoly, but it is also one of the Corporal Works of Mercy, perhaps the hardest to follow.

People in jail don't get a lot of sympathy. They have violated society's rules, have even hurt someone or worse. But they remain human beings who are owed decent treatment, counseling, and respect. That is the Christian imperative, Christ's directive to love your neighbor as yourself.

Never been in a jail? They aren't nice places. Most are very clean, sterile even, with nothing to provide a hint that someone actually cares about the prisoners' spiritual well-being. Most Catholic dioceses have a structured prison ministry with chaplains and other assigned ministers. Usually the service is provided by a religious sister or brother or a deacon or priest. Those clerical people can be screened for security by prison officials more easily than laymen. Nevertheless, the prison chaplains often need assistance from laymen at Mass or other liturgical services, at scriptural study, and at nonreligious activities such as tutoring, counseling, teaching life skills, or

preparing inmates to be tested for their general educational diplomas (GED).

Sister Helen Prejean of the Sisters of St. Joseph took Jesus' mandate to visit the imprisoned to heroic lengths. She was spiritual adviser to men condemned to death. Her experiences led her to write a book about her ministry, *Dead Man Walking*, and it became a bestseller. It later was made into a notion picture.

Catholics should look into this challenging ministry by consulting with the local diocese to learn what help the prison chaplains need and how to bring that help and caring to people who feel a long way from human compassion and the mercy of God's love.

51. Bury the Dead

"Bring out yer dead. Bring out yer dead." The chant from the dark, satirical comedy film *Monty Python and the Holy Grail* is actually the seventh of the Corporal Works of Mercy. Generations ago, death was a more common occurrence. Plagues and infectious diseases could kill large numbers of people quickly. Bodies piled up because family members were too sick, too traumatized, or already dead themselves. The burden of giving Christian burials fell on the community.

In the modern world of preventive medicine and treatable diseases, those group deaths are uncommon. Funerals are institutionalized and part of a commercial industry. The Christian imperative to give dignity to the dead remains, however. Catholics should ensure that their dead friends and

relatives receive proper and dignified funerals and burials. And what about those who die with no resources, no relatives, no close friends to provide them proper burial and to mourn them? They get buried in a pauper's cemetery, but there is usually no funeral service. Although we may not know when such people on the margins of society die and are buried, Catholics can nevertheless include the homeless dead who have no family in our prayers for the dead at Mass and on other occasions, such as on All Souls Day.

There is a popular subculture in the entertainment world, the phenomenon of monster trucks, the vehicles with big wheels that roll over everything and do amazing acrobatics. One of the most popular performers is a truck named "Grave Digger." Think about that; a monster truck as a symbolic manifestation of the Christian duty to bury the dead.

52. Serve as an Acolyte

In the "old days," there were altar boys, school-age boys who donned miniature cassocks and white surplices (the tunic over the cassock) and dutifully assisted the priest during Mass and other liturgical events. They learned to mutter the prayer responses in garbled, phonetic Latin, even if they weren't sure of the meaning. Some wayward altar boys were known to swig a sample of the altar wine in the sacristy while Father wasn't looking. (It was sweet and not very good.) Including altar boys in liturgical services was considered a good introduction to the rituals of the Church as a way to instill interest in becoming a priest.

No girls allowed! In fact, females were not supposed be in the sanctuary, the area around the altar, during Mass. One wondered what the priest or bishop would do if Mary, Jesus' mother, showed up and walked up to the altar. Since those misogynistic days of yore, a more inclusive, Christian attitude changed Church policy, and girls and women have been welcomed as altar servers, lectors at Mass, and Extraordinary Ministers of Holy Communion. Now anyone of any age is eligible to serve as what used to be called an altar boy. And they don't have to learn to mutter in Latin that they probably would not understand. Church parishes that have a parochial school continue to use students, boys and

girls, as the primary source of what are called "acolytes," as a way to make the liturgy more inclusive of children, but adults also become acolytes. Every Catholic should have the opportunity to be an acolyte.

53. Gather for Eucharistic Adoration

The usual practice in most Catholic churches is to keep the hosts, the bread wafers consecrated at Mass, in a tabernacle near the altar. The presence of the body and blood of Jesus stored therein is typically marked by a lighted red candle that burns continuously. Periodically, the faithful gather in church when Mass is not being celebrated to worship Christ in his real presence. During those periods, the consecrated hosts are removed from the obscurity of the tabernacle and put on display in a vessel called the ciborium for prayer and adoration. Groups of parishioners meet at the church for communal prayers and for individual meditation.

Some parishes will conduct Eucharistic adoration as a "holy hour," during which the worshipers' prayers will focus on a specified topic, such as prayers for the sick, relief from drought, for peace, and so forth. There are specific guidelines for the rituals of exposing and worshiping the Eucharist with which Catholics can become familiar and make the experience of adoration and the holy hour more meaningful.

Although not as prevalent as it once was, the Forty Hours Devotion is another manifestation of worship of the Eucharist outside of the tabernacle. The Forty Hours Devotion is a period of continual prayer in the church where the sacrament is exposed. Parishioners sign up for specific times to be in church in prayer, including in the early morning. There will be group devotions, preaching by a visiting deacon or priest, and special Masses. The number forty connects the devotion to the many instances in the Bible in which that number is mentioned: the forty days and nights of the flood, the Hebrews' forty years' wandering in the desert, Jesus' forty days of prayer and fasting in preparation for his ministry.

54. Join the St. Vincent de Paul Society

In 1833 some devout French laymen formed an organization to serve the poor, in answer to the challenges Jesus made in the Gospels. They chose St. Vincent as their inspiration, a holy man of the seventeenth century who had devoted his life to serving the poor. The organization spread across the world, and today most larger parishes have chapters. The society consists of laymen who organize service and goods to the poor people of their parish, diocese, and community.

The rules of the society prohibit the discussion of politics at meetings, which is the time for prayer and for planning their service to the poor. The rules also require precise record-keeping so that the goods and funds distributed are properly accounted for. Records of each family being served are kept to ensure that the help provided is directed at the specific need being served as well as to protect the privacy of the poor. St Vincent made it clear that Christians are the servants of the poor and that the poor deserve dignity and compassion.

The St. Vincent de Paul Society is a place where Catholics from all levels of the social order get together to make their commitment to Christianity physically manifest. The truck driver, the salesperson, and the waitress are on the same level of service with the professionals and the managers. In joining and participating in the works of the St. Vincent de Paul Society, Catholics can respond to the requirements of the Corporal Works of Mercy and the call of Jesus and the scripture to serve the poor.

In St. Matthew's gospel, Jesus says, "The poor you will always have with you." Get out there and take care of them.

55. Join the Holy Name Society

Another worldwide organization of Catholics, the Holy Name Society has been part of Catholicism since the Middle Ages. Its members pledge to support the teachings of the Catholic Church and to respect the name of Jesus. In the Divine Praises recited after Benediction, the second recitation, after "Blessed be God," is "Blessed be His Holy Name."

The members pledge to refrain from blasphemy and cursing and immoral speech in general. Chapters of the Holy Name Society are formed in each church parish, and one of the requirements of members is that they attend Mass and receive Holy Communion as a group at least once every three months. Most chapters meet for Mass on the second Sunday of each month, a day designated "Holy Name Sunday."

Originally the Holy Name Society was for men only, but today it includes women as well. Perhaps in the "old days" no one wanted to admit that "ladies" swore too. In a culture in which the public discourse has become increasingly coarse and vulgar, with much language on television being "bleeped" by the modern version of social censors, the Holy Name Society's mission is particularly appropriate. "Watch your language!" has a spiritual component too. Who can last a full week or even a full day without using vulgar and profane language? The Holy Name Society isn't just for old guys in musty suits.

The society conducts charitable work as well as spiritual devotions, all to contribute to their pledge to serve the institutional Church.

56. Serve in the Altar Society

Every Catholic parish used to have a Ladies' Altar Society, an organization of laywomen who kept the altar and the sanctuary spiffy and tidy, with clean altar linens and fresh flowers on appropriate Sundays and feast days. Before there were so many ministries open to laypeople, it was an opportunity for women to serve the church in a way that was important to the liturgy. Today many more ministries are available for laywomen—men too—and altar society participation has dwindled in recent years. Nevertheless, the society, which does not exclude men although most active members are women, still provides an important service.

Candle wax and ashes regularly find their way to the altar coverings. The various cloth items need to be washed, usually by hand, and ironed before the next use. The cloth covering the altar, the equivalent of a tablecloth, is the first level. Then a square linen cloth, about the size of a dinner napkin, goes in the center of the altar as a place for the chalice and other vessels holding the bread and wine to be consecrated. A smaller cloth, the equivalent of a napkin, is draped across the chalice and is used to clean and dry it after communion. It is called the purificator. A stiff, square, cloth covering for the chalice is used in some churches. It is the pall. And there is sometimes a cloth veil that covers the chalice as Mass begins and the vessels at the end of Mass.

There will be a towel the priest uses in the ceremonial washing of his hands before the offertory of the Mass, and there will be additional purificators used by ministers of Holy Communion to wipe the chalices after each communicant receives the sacrament. Lipstick and spittle are wiped away onto the purificators, which must be cleaned before the next service.

There are regular laundry needs for the church. Everyone can help.

57. Become a Eucharistic Minister

The official title of a layperson who has been designated and trained to distribute Holy Communion is Extraordinary Minister of Holy Communion (EMHC). Usually such a person is called by the shorthand term "Eucharistic Minister." Being an EMHC/ Eucharistic Minister is an opportunity for laymen and women to participate in the holiest part of the Mass, the distribution of the consecrated bread and wine to the faithful of the congregation.

The ministers are "extraordinary" because, under Church law, the ordained men—that is, the bishops, priests, and deacons—are the "ordinary" ministers of the sacraments. In addition to distributing the Eucharist at Mass, EMHCs also bring communion to people who are physically unable to attend Mass, such as homebound or hospitalized Catholics.

Becoming a Eucharistic Minister is not difficult. Each minister must go through a training session on the proper procedures for approaching the altar, receiving the vessels containing the consecrated bread and wine, and distributing the sacrament properly and reverently to the faithful. Preparation and training are also accompanied by prayer and reflection on the significance of the Eucharist in Catholicism.

The consecrated bread is given either on the communicant's tongue or in the hand. Some communicants may want to take the wafer and dip it into the consecrated wine, a practice called by the very Church-sounding term "intinction." This practice is discouraged by rules of the Conference of Bishops.

And all Eucharistic Ministers need to learn what to do when the host falls to the floor or into a communicant's clothing. (Suggestion: tell the priest.) Sometimes reverence gets awkward.

58. Become an Oblate

Never heard of Oblates? They are what can be described as associate members of religious orders, Catholics who live their regular lives in work and family but make a promise to connect them to religious orders whose members take formal vows, live in community, and follow the traditions of their respective orders. A Catholic, male or female, can be a fully professed member of the Order of St. Benedict, the Benedictines, and have the suffix "O.S.B." after one's name. Lay Catholics can become Oblates of St. Benedict by making a formal association with a monastery and participating in the work and prayer of the monks or nuns. Novelist Walker Percy was an Oblate of St. Benedict associated with St. Joseph's Abbey in Louisiana. He is buried in the monks' cemetery on the monastery grounds.

To make it confusing, there are Oblates of other religious orders who take formal, full vows and can be ordained. The Missionary Oblates of Mary Immaculate is one of those organizations. If you read a priest's or a brother's name with "O.M.I." as a suffix, he is a professed member. The late archbishop of Chicago, Cardinal Francis George, was an Oblate of Mary Immaculate. Other religious orders of Oblates whose members are consecrated, taking formal vows, are Oblates of St. Francis de Sales (O.S.F.S.), Oblates of St. Joseph (O.S.J.), and Oblates of the Virgin Mary (O.V.M.).

Want some more confusion? The term "oblate" when used in the name of a religious organization comes from the Latin verb *oblatus*, past participle of the word meaning "to offer"; but *oblatus* can also mean "lengthen" and is the base of the English adjective "oblate," as in "oblate spheroid." The earth is somewhat flattened at its poles, making it an "oblate spheroid," on which Oblates of the Catholic Church work and pray. Catholics, confused and otherwise, have the opportunity to become consecrated or lay Oblates, without being flattened.

59. Join the Knights of Columbus

The Knights of Columbus are almost everywhere in Catholicism. Founded as a fraternal, charitable, and service organization in Connecticut in 1882, the Knights are spread throughout the Catholic world. At the time of founding, Masonic fraternal orders were vigorous and numerous in the United States. Many of them were openly and aggressively anti-Catholic. Nevertheless, becoming a Mason was often almost necessary for a man to advance socially, politically, and financially in America of that era and into the twentieth century. A faithful Catholic businessman was not welcome in Masonic lodges.

Furthermore, the Catholic Church officially prohibits Catholics from joining or associating with Masonic orders because the Church views Freemasonry as a naturalistic religion in conflict with Catholic theology. The Knights of Columbus provide Catholics with a fraternal organization with similar forms. The Knights promise service to the Church and charitable services to the needy. It is also a life insurance company, in keeping with its original mission of providing for widows and orphans of its members. As a fraternal society, the members support each other socially, ethically, and with business connections. The Knights also mimic some of the colorful rituals of the Masons, sporting capes, swords, and plumed hats at funerals and other religious services. Although the practice is waning, some Knights wear decorated fezzes, obviously copied from the Masons' charitable wing, the Shriners.

The Knights remain an all-male organization, and, like the Masons, some of their official meetings are secret. Some female auxiliary spin-offs were founded, but their numbers seem to be dwindling. There are the Columbiettes, the Catholic Daughters of the Americas, and the Daughters of Isabella. (Get it? Isabella was the queen of Spain who financed Columbus's voyages to America.)

Even if joining the Knights of Columbus is not your cup of tea, you can join them in their charitable work and in their mission to defend Catholicism against attacks that continue to surface in contemporary society.

60. Join a Third Order

There are Oblates who are laypeople who associate formally with a religious order such as the Benedictines. There are other groups of laymen and women who are in a similar relationship with other religious orders. They are called Third Orders or Third Orders Secular. Like the Oblates, they provide an opportunity for Catholics who live regular lives outside of a monastery or convent to become a member and to participate in the mission and life of the order. The best known is the Third Order of St. Francis (Franciscans), but there are Third Orders of Mt. Carmel (Carmelites) and St. Dominic (Dominicans).

If there are Third Orders, who or what are the First and Second? The First Orders are the male friars who may be priests or brothers, wear the habit of their order, and live in community. The Second Orders are the nuns who have taken formal vows, wear the habit, and live in community. Within the Third Orders—and some of the First and Second Orders— there are even more differentiated communities under the designation of Franciscan, Carmelite, Dominican. For example, in the Franciscans there are, among others, Capuchin Friars and Recollect Friars. It is sometimes said that only God knows how many different branches and subdivisions of religious orders there are, and even he scratches his head from time to time.

Nevertheless, the Third Orders are an opportunity for all Catholics to participate in the life of a religious order without actually making formal vows and without wearing a habit.

61. Be a Church Usher

There is a singer-songwriter named Usher and a horror short story by Edgar Allan Poe called "The Fall of the House of Usher," but those are not what Catholics think of when they attend Sunday Mass. Church ushers open the church before Mass. They greet people coming to Mass, even those who arrive late. They make newcomers feel welcome. Inside the church they distribute Mass booklets, weekly bulletins, and flyers advertising special events at the parish. Ushers make sure everyone has a seat in a pew. They escort parents with noisy or fidgety children to the church's vestibule or "cry room," if there is one. They show Mass-goers who feel the call of nature where the restrooms are located.

After the homily and recitation of the Creed, ushers perform one of their most important duties: passing the baskets to collect the weekly offering from the congregation. Because this function comes shortly after the homily, being an usher is an excuse for retiring to the rear of the church to avoid a boring sermon.

Ushers are often entrusted with counting the collection and separating cash from checks and envelopes, making sure the special collections are kept separate from the general ones. Next, during communion, ushers ensure the orderly procession of communicants to receive the sacrament, assisting the elderly and the disabled.

After Mass, the ushers distribute the parish bulletin and other literature as the congregation leaves the church. Being an usher allows a Catholic to move around and do physical activity during Mass, not just sitting passively in the pew. It's a good way to get to know the members of the parish.

62. Sing in the Choir

Everybody can sing. After all, we belt out Christmas carols every year, even without the stimulation of spiked eggnog (although it helps). In most parishes, singing in the choir is much like singing Christmas carols, just with different tunes and lyrics. Larger parishes may attract more musically trained and inclined members, but people who just like to sing are usually welcome too.

"Sing to the Lord a new song; sing to the Lord, all the earth" (*Psalms* 96:1). St. Paul and his friend Silas were singing even while they were in jail (*Acts* 16:25). You see, the scriptures are telling you to get out there and sing in the church choir.

Many Catholics get their introduction to choir music when they are children and join (or get drafted into) the Catholic school choir. It's a good place to start; nobody, especially parents, expects their children to sing particularly well. The participation in a group liturgical activity is the main point in singing in the school choir. When some of the boys' voices begin to crack as puberty approaches, the resulting giggles and snickers may cause embarrassment and can be the signal to the young men that they are no longer children. But the experience of singing in the children's choir is fine preparation and inspiration for joining an adult choir later in life, as one matures and the voice settles down.

Depending on local practice, the parish choir may sing the *Kyrie Eleison* in Greek and the *Agnus Dei* in Latin. Give it a try; try out for the choir.

63. Volunteer to Be a Lector at Mass

You have probably attended a Mass at which the person(s) reading the scriptural passages before the deacon or priest reads the Gospel is almost unintelligible. Some lectors read too fast, some stumble over unfamiliar words in the readings, some have voices that lack the tone and strength to be heard and understood. This is your opportunity. You can volunteer to be a lector at Mass. Reading the scripture aloud clearly and distinctly is an important ministry. The inspired words of the Lord come from the lector's mouth. In order for listeners to understand what the scriptures are teaching, it is important that the lector be clear and coherent. Hundreds of years ago, the position of lector was only for men on the path to ordination. Now any layperson can proclaim the scriptural passages of the day.

This isn't easy for many people. There may be a tendency to rush the readings, to "get through" what Isaiah or St. Paul has to say that day. Training and practice help, with the knowledge that what the lector is saying may be the only message from the Bible that some members of the congregation will hear. Prepare for the readings well before Mass; ask for guidance on how to pronounce some of those Old Testament names properly. Slow down, enunciate the words carefully, make eye contact with the congregation. This should be a happy experience for them as well as for the lector.

When you inform people that you are a lector at Mass, be sure to pronounce the short o. If the sound comes out "lecter" rather than "lector," people unfamiliar with the liturgical meaning may think that you are identifying with the evil psychopath of fiction and film, Hannibal Lecter.

64. Read Spiritual Literature

Catholics can and should advance their knowledge and appreciation of their religion by reading what some of the many profound thinkers have written. Catholicism has been around for a couple of thousand years, and during that time a lot of important and inspiring materials have been written. You can't read all of it, some of it is very dense, but there is much to choose from.

One of the most influential writers in the history of Catholicism is St. Augustine of Hippo, who wrote in the fourth century. His *City of God* and *Confessions* molded Christian theology into a form that lasted. In the nineteenth century, St. John Henry Newman, an English cardinal, was a prolific spiritual writer whose work is probably more accessible to modern Catholics than St. Augustine's. Newman's religious autobiography, *Apologia Pro Vita Sua* (*Explanation for My Life*), is easily read, a classic of Christian spirituality. He was also a poet, and his *The Idea of A University* influenced what higher education is supposed to do.

Photograph by Anne Renouf, courtesy of the Jubilee Museum, Columbus, Ohio

Popular American Catholic writers of the twentieth century are Thomas Merton, a Trappist monk, and Bishop Fulton Sheen, who pioneered the use of television to proclaim the teachings of the Catholic Church. Both writers are easy to read and inspiring. Merton's spiritual autobiography, *The Seven Storey Mountain*, published in 1948, was a bestseller on the *New York Times* list. The book has been called a modern version of St. Augustine's *Confessions*. Really challenging to casual readers is the theology of Fr. Karl Rahner, a twentieth-century Jesuit theologian. He is considered the most influential Catholic theologian of the twentieth century. His works are not for the faint of heart, however. The writing is in very dense German, so dense that someone quipped that even God would have trouble following his thoughts.

Much easier to read are the simple, pious meditations of St. Therese of Lisieux, a French Carmelite nun of the nineteenth century, known as the Little Flower of Jesus. She was ordered by her Mother Superior, who recognized her holiness, to write her meditations. They were published as *The Story of a Soul* and continue to inspire readers.

65. Read Catholic Fiction

Catholic fiction has been around almost as long as fiction writing itself. A modern Catholic should delve into reading one or more of the great writers who use Catholicism as part of their novels or are strongly influenced by their religion. Some of the best of this genre are British. The amazingly prolific G. K. Chesterton is known for, among his many accomplishments, a series of short stories featuring one Father Brown, a priest who is also a detective. Chesterton influenced a British atheist, C. S. Lewis, to become a Catholic, and Lewis's novel *The Screwtape Letters* shows how thoroughly he took to Catholicism.

Another British novelist of the twentieth century is Graham Greene, whose writing shows both the strong influence of Catholicism and the author's struggles with it. His 1940 novel, *The Power and the Glory*, features a deeply flawed priest on the run from persecutors during the Mexican revolution.

American Catholic writers include Flannery O'Connor, an eccentric novelist who spent her life in the rural South. She was surrounded and somewhat influenced by Protestants, but her Catholicism figures strongly in her writings. In a collection of her short stories, *A Good Man Is Hard to Find and Other Stories,* her Catholicism comes through loud and clear.

Another American Catholic novelist, a winner of the National Book Award for fiction, is Walker Percy, a convert to Catholicism. His writings are heavily influenced by his Catholicism, including *The Second Coming* and *The Thanatos Syndrome.* Percy's novel *Love in the Ruins* is subtitled *The Adventures of a Bad Catholic at a Time Near the End of the World.*

As the cliché goes, curl up with a good book by a Catholic author and be entertained and inspired.

Did you know that J. R. R. Tolkien, author of the world's bestselling work of fiction, *The Lord of the Rings,* was a devout Catholic?

66. Say the Rosary

Among the many physical items immediately identifiable as "Catholic" is the rosary. The string of beads for counting prayers is a visible sign of one's Catholicism. Catholics and non-Catholics alike drape a rosary in vehicles and homes as some type of devotion and for protection, even if they don't use it for prayer. Undertakers routinely place rosaries in the hands of Catholic cadavers, whether the deceased ever recited the rosary or not. The rosary identifies the corpse as Catholic and provides a hope that the departed will be noticed favorably as the soul struggles to get to heaven.

The word "rosary" derives from the Latin *rosarius,* a string of roses. Popular belief, without much historical support, attributes the rosary to St. Dominic in the thirteenth century, after a message from Our Lady, as a prayer against heretics.

In case you've forgotten or haven't said the rosary in a very long time, it consists of five sets of repetitious prayers counted on the physical rosary after introductory recitation of the Apostles' Creed, the Our Father, and three Hail Marys. Each of the five sets begins with the Lord's Prayer, followed by ten Hail Marys. At the end of each of the sets, called "decades," the Doxology is recited. ("Glory be to the Father. . . . ") Each decade of the rosary is assigned a meditation called a "mystery." These have nothing to do with mystery novels or their ilk. The mysteries of the rosary are meditations on events in the life of Jesus or Mary and are in four sets: the Joyful Mysteries for Mondays and Saturdays, the Sorrowful Mysteries for Tuesdays and Fridays, the Glorious Mysteries for Wednesdays and Sundays, and the Mysteries of Light for Thursdays. If you've forgotten what the twenty mysteries are, go get yourself a booklet and a rosary, and take a lap around the beads.

67. Travel with St. Christopher

Poor St. Christopher! He got demoted, purged in the reforms following the Second Vatican Council. Despite his popularity as the patron saint of travelers and the millions of medals that had been placed in vehicles, the story of the early Christian martyr carrying a child on his shoulders as he waded across a river is a fable; no historical record of his existence could be found. Were all those medals and prayers to the saint before setting out on a journey a waste of breath?

Even if the legendary saint did not exist, there was in historical fact a St. Christopher who was a martyr of the early Christian Church. Further, prayer is prayer, regardless of which saint is invoked, and all prayer ultimately goes to God.

The saint's name is a combination of two Greek words (he was a Greek) meaning "Christ-bearer." Christopher was a Christian but apparently not a particularly enthusiastic one. The legend of the child on his shoulders is that as Christopher, a large, muscular man whose day job was carrying travelers across a stream—they paid him to stay dry—was wading through the stream with a child on his shoulders, ordinarily an easy trip, the child became exceedingly heavy. The child revealed himself as Jesus and, to prove it, ordered the ferryman to plant his staff in the ground. The planted staff sprouted branches, and Christopher was convinced. He was later beheaded as a Christian martyr. It's a fine story, even if it's not factually based.

Nevertheless, a St. Christopher medal in your car or truck or boat or airplane is a reminder that a prayer before, during, and even after a journey is a good idea.

68. Pray to St. Anthony for Lost Things

Your mobile phone is missing. Where are the keys that you thought were in your purse? What became of that important document you picked up at the lawyer's office? Quick! Say a prayer to St. Anthony, patron saint of lost stuff. Although there are several saints named Anthony, the popular saint of lost things is the thirteenth-century Franciscan friar, St. Anthony of Padua.

Why Anthony became the saint to whom prayer is directed

when material items are lost is based on thievery. A disillusioned novice in the monastery stole Anthony's prayer book as he was skipping town and abandoning religious life. Unable to locate his book, Anthony prayed to find it. Something happened to make the larcenous novice come back to the monastery and return the book. Anthony and the friars saw this repentance as an act of God and reinstated the chastened young man. Immediately following Anthony's death, people started invoking his assistance when they lost things, often with quick results. The practice continues into contemporary times, even among people who are not Catholic or even religious in any way.

St. Anthony remains one of the most popular saints of all time. Some churches have statues of him, and at his feet is where churchgoers leave items found in the church: rosaries, eyeglasses, keys. If you left something in church, check with St. Anthony.

Here's a quick prayer, two versions, when an item is lost:

> Dear St. Anthony,
> Please come around.
> Something is lost
> And cannot be found.

And the flippant version:

> Tony, Tony,
> Look around.
> Something's lost
> And must be found.

Prayers to St. Anthony are for lost material things. Don't try to stretch the prayer to include lost opportunity, lost innocence, or losing one's cool.

69. Wear a Medal and Chain

Everybody in show business seems to be wearing a cross and chain. Rock musicians, pop singers, and bluesmen like to have the image of Jesus hanging around their necks. Rap performers in attire not unlike a pimp's wardrobe strut about with crosses hanging. People who have only the vaguest notion of who Jesus is nevertheless adorn themselves with crosses and crucifixes as some sort of amulet or hocus-pocus protection. Or maybe the symbol is meaningless to the wearer, nothing more than a fashion statement.

For Catholics a medal and chain is a physical mark of identification, like a security badge or a soldier's dog tags. It reminds the wearer and shows an observer that she or he is Catholic, a follower of Christ. The crosses and crucifixes come in a great variety of styles and sizes, so a Catholic has a lot of choice.

There are many other medals available with stylized likenesses of the Blessed Mother and various saints, well known and obscure. Very popular is the Miraculous Medal of Our Lady. In 1830 the Blessed Virgin appeared to a French nun and in those apparitions gave instructions on what should appear on a medal with her likeness. Those medals are available in Catholic book and gift stores. Lots of saints' medals can be found there too, along with medals depicting guardian angels and the Holy Spirit.

If you have a devotion to a particular saint or are looking for a medal of your patron saint, you can probably find it. Medals and chains make fine gifts too. Get a medal and chain and wear it as a physical symbol of your Catholicism. But first present it to a priest or deacon for it to be blessed. Then it is ready to wear, with a special meaning not found in a cross hanging from a rock performer's neck.

70. Collect and Distribute Holy Pictures and Prayer Cards

Back when Catholics carried the big *St. Joseph Missal* to Mass, everybody collected Holy Pictures. They made nice bookmarks in the missals and were good references for quick prayers. Catholic schoolchildren got them from their teachers; they were passed around at Baptisms, First Communions, and Confirmations. Although the practice has waned somewhat, particularly since the decline in the use of personal missals, Holy Pictures with prayers on the reverse side are still popular at funerals. Undertakers provide them with the name of the deceased and a prayer, along with a standard, popular picture of Jesus or Mary.

Catholic book and gift stores often have an amazing variety of Holy Pictures and Prayer Cards. Some are of very obscure saints or saints with a particular ethnic connection. There is a Holy Picture with the image of the legendary St. Expedite. He is depicted as a baby-faced Roman soldier holding a banner inscribed with *Hodie*, the Latin word for "today." He tramples a serpent marked *Cras,* Latin for "tomorrow." Whether St. Expedite was real is debatable, but his Holy Picture is interesting.

There are Holy Pictures with dedications to dozens of titles of the Blessed Mother. Our Lady, Queen of Peace; Mother of Sorrows; Our Lady of Divine Providence; Mary, Recourse of Sinners are just a few of the names available. Catholics would do well to browse the gift and book shops or online and acquire some cards for distribution on family occasions or to continue the tradition of the cards at Baptism and other sacraments.

If a friend is in the hospital or otherwise laid up from illness or injury, give that friend some spiritual support by bringing a Holy Picture to the bedside. Prayers can go a long way to heal the sick and the injured. Besides, Holy Pictures and Prayer Cards are cheaper than flowers.

71. Put Crucifixes and Statues in Your Home

Another practice that identifies you as Catholic is to put into your home a visible reminder, an identification with Catholicism. The way to do this is by hanging a crucifix on the wall, over the doorway, in the kitchen. Catholicism uses crucifixes much more than other Christian denominations; most do not use them at all. Let's not forget what the crucifix is for: it is a reminder that Jesus Christ died while hanging on a cross and, in doing so, sacrificed himself so that all other human beings could be redeemed, reconciled with God.

A crucifix on the wall of your home is a call to prayer. A glance at the figure should quickly bring a prayer or spiritual thought to mind. Some Catholics will place a crucifix in every room, maybe even the bathrooms, all to remind of the presence of God and as a call to prayer.

It's not just the crucifix. Many Catholic homes have statues to one or more saints or the Blessed Mother; a personal patron, for example, a saint to whom the house is dedicated; or a saint connected to one's heritage. St. Patrick for an Irish-American family and Our Lady of Guadalupe for a Mexican-American family are examples.

The practice of statues in the home is quite ancient and actually predates Christianity. In classical times, in the homes of the Romans were shrines with small figurines of that family's personal deities, their "household gods." There would be a figurine of Janus, protector of the doorway, and Vesta, goddess of the hearth. The Romans also had small statues of the spirits of their ancestors. It was not a great leap to transfer that pagan practice into the Christian observances still in practice today.

If you don't have a crucifix or statues in your home, get one or more. They will mark you as Catholic to yourself, your family, your visitors.

72. Place Madonnas in the Yard (and Other Saints)

Maybe there are people who place statues to Mary and the saints in their front yards who are not Catholics, but they are definitely outnumbered by those who are. Passing a house with a Mary statue in front immediately makes you think that whoever lives there is One of Us.

There is a sameness in all those statues. Typically Mary is portrayed as standing, dressed in a long gown, a flowing cape, and a headscarf. Her eyes focus downward, indicating that she is deep in prayer. Her arms are at a slight angle from her body, palms outward. This is a statuary copy of the many paintings of the Blessed Mother showing beams of light flowing out of her hands, symbolic of the graces she bestows on the human race.

Some of the yard statues become shrines, with statues of children kneeling and praying, a representation of Our Lady's apparitions at Fatima in Portugal. If the Madonna statue is accompanied by a fountain or a pool, the homeowner may be commemorating Our Lady of Lourdes and the healing waters there.

Although Mary seems to be the most popular choice for yard statues, she is not the only one. The most popular saint of Christians of all persuasions is most likely St. Francis of Assisi, the friar who is said to have given sermons to the birds and the animals when people wouldn't listen to him. St. Francis must be the unofficial patron saint of birdbaths because many landscape vendors have the devices ready to sell, with the holy man holding a big bowl and welcoming the birds.

Statues of Jesus in flowing robes with his hands above his head are popular too. Although the gesture could be interpreted as the Lord getting exasperated, the statue has been called, irreverently, "Touchdown Jesus." Nevertheless, the statues in the yard, like the ones in the house, are reminders.

73. Bury St. Joseph

St. Joseph doesn't get left out of the yard, but you might not see him. His statue could be buried somewhere around the "For Sale" sign. This isn't an officially approved Catholic devotion, but lots of Catholics—and people who aren't Catholic—use a statue of St. Joseph to help sell a house. It's a superstition, really, but, like many superstitions, lots of people think it works. Real estate agents carry small statues of St. Joseph with them in case a client is interested. (If the house has been on the market a long time, the agent may secretly bury one for extra help.)

Here's how it's done. Obtain a small statue of St. Joseph at a religious supply store; three or four inches high is a good size. The store may even have kits with instructions on how to bury.

1. Wrap the statue in a cloth and a plastic bag to protect it from the dirt.

2. Dig a hole deep enough to hold the statue and be covered with dirt. The hole should be near the "For Sale" sign. If there's no yard, use a flower or shrub pot with something growing in it.

3. Put St. Joseph into the hole *upside down* vertically, facing the house.

4. Cover the hole with dirt.

5. Say a prayer to St. Joseph.

6. As soon as the contract of sale has been signed, dig up the statue and move it to a place of reverence in your new home.

7. Make a prayer of thanksgiving to St. Joseph.

8. Don't mention any of this to your parish priest.

74. Wear a Scapular

Unlike the practice of wearing a cross and chain, the wearing of a scapular by non-Catholics has never caught on. In fact, there really aren't a lot of Catholics who observe the devotion either. First, a little background. The word "scapular" comes from the Latin word for shoulders. Originally it was part of monks' habit, their uniform. It still is worn by many in monastic orders, including the Benedictines. It is a narrow panel worn over the habit through which the wearer puts his head so that the panels flow down the back and the front.

Over centuries it was adopted by other religious orders and by laypeople who were in some formal association with an order, such as Oblates and members of the Third Orders. These orders were, among others, the Carmelites, the Servites, the Trinitarians, the Franciscans, the Dominicans, and the Mercedarians. (Never heard of the Mercedarians? They were an order founded in the thirteenth century by St. Peter Nolasco with the mission to rescue Christians captured by the Moors.)

Today the laity can wear a scapular in the form of small pieces of cloth imprinted with an illustration of a saint, Jesus, or the Blessed Mother, similar to the practice of wearing a medal and chain. The small scapular, inspired by the original large one, is in two parts, one for the chest, one for the back, connected by cords to be worn around the neck under clothing. Although it is usually worn by laymen and women who have associated with religious orders, anyone can wear one. Many of the small scapulars display on one of the panels the message from Our Lady that "Whoever dies wearing this scapular shall not suffer eternal fire." It is a powerful promise, enough to make you go buy a scapular and wear it.

75. Visit the National Shrine of the Immaculate Conception

Since at least medieval times, pilgrimages have been part of Catholicism. In the fourteenth century, Geoffrey Chaucer wrote *The Canterbury Tales* about pilgrims who were journeying to the shrine of St. Thomas à Becket in Canterbury, England, and told stories to each other to pass the time. American Catholics should continue the tradition of pilgrimages by visiting the big

church in Washington, D.C., called the Basilica of the National Shrine of the Immaculate Conception.

In 1847, at the request of the American bishops, Pope Pius IX dedicated the United States to the Blessed Mother in her title of the Immaculate Conception. There were plans in the works to build a huge church as a national shrine, but, like the great cathedrals of Europe, decades passed as plans were made and changed, funds raised, and construction proceeded in stages. The basilica is built in the style of a medieval European cathedral, only bigger. Parts of the shrine opened as early as 1920 for Mass and other liturgical services, but it was not completed until 1959. In fact, work continues on the shrine, so that with regular modifications it may never be completely "complete."

The basilica stands as the largest church in North America and, according to its website, is "one of the ten largest churches in the world." This is probably debatable, but does size really matter when devotion to the Blessed Mother is involved?

Some Catholics consider the shrine to be beautiful and inspiring; others think it is too big, too lavish, too triumphal. Some Catholics, priests included, like to joke that Our Lady appeared in the big church, looked around, then said to worshipers, "I want you to build a beautiful church on this site."

Go see for yourself. Make your own pilgrimage and form an opinion about the National Shrine.

76. Visit Other National Shrines

There's not just one. Although the big basilica in Washington, D.C., is *the* national shrine, there are others throughout the country dedicated to other saints and in honor of other titles of the Blessed Mother. In Philadelphia is the National Shrine to St. Rita of Cascia, patron saint of battered women. The first American-born saint, St. Elizabeth Ann Seton, is honored at her national shrine in Emmitsburg, Maryland, northwest of Baltimore. She was a mother and widow at age twenty-nine, but her energy and holiness led her to start an order of nuns.

St. Therese of Lisieux, a very popular saint known as the Little Flower of Jesus, is commemorated at the National Shrine of the Little Flower Basilica in Royal Oak, Michigan. Also in the Midwest is the National Shrine of the Cathedral of St. Paul in— where else?—St. Paul, Minnesota.

St. Ann or St. Anne or St. Anna was the mother of the Blessed Virgin and is so popular in Catholic devotion that there are several national shrines dedicated to her in the United States. One is in Scranton, Pennsylvania; one is in Metairie, Louisiana, near New Orleans; another in the church of Our Lady of Fatima in Chicago; and yet another in the small village of St. Anne (appropriate name) near Kankakee, Illinois.

Illinois Catholics have great fondness for shrines; in Belleville is the National Shrine of Our Lady of the Snows, staffed by the Oblates of Mary Immaculate and described as a place of hope and healing. The Holy Mother is again honored at the National Shrine of Our Lady of LaSalette in Attleboro, Massachusetts.

Of course, the National Shrine of St. Francis of Assisi is in San Francisco, California.

St. Jude, one of the apostles also called Thaddeus, is the patron saint of hopeless causes. If you're running out of hope, visit one of his national shrines and offer prayers. There's one in Chicago and one in New Orleans.

77. Make a Pilgrimage to Rome and the Vatican

One of the requirements of being a good Muslim is to perform the Hadj at least once in life. The Hadj is a pilgrimage to Islam's holiest place, Mecca, and a series of required actions and devotions. There's no similar requirement in Catholicism, but Catholics who are physically and financially able to do so should visit Rome and the Vatican at least once.

Getting an audience with the pope isn't hard to do. You go to the bronze gate at St. Peter's and ask the Swiss Guard on duty for a form to request an audience. These audiences are free, but you'll be with a lot of other people. A private, one-on-one meeting with the Holy Father requires some connection. Knowing a Rome-based priest or bishop helps. Maybe you know someone who knows one of the pope's bodyguards, the Swiss Guard, the men in those striped sixteenth-century uniforms. A guy who wears one of those suits and carries a halberd at work ought to have some pull with somebody. Even if you can't arrange a private or group meeting with the pope, you can join the throngs in St. Peter's Square on Sundays when the pope appears in a huge window and blesses the crowd. You can say you had an audience with the pope—along with several thousand others who came for the blessing.

In the Vatican you are at the heart of Catholicism, an independent city-state whose chief executive is the Vicar of Christ and wields enormous influence throughout the world. St. Peter's Basilica is the largest church in the world. Inside are great works of art; beneath the church are the tombs of St. Peter and many other popes. The nearby Sistine Chapel is not just the place where cardinals gather to elect a new pope; it is one of the most inspiring works of art in the world.

Beyond the Vatican is Rome, for two thousand years the cultural center of Western Civilization. There are many important Christian churches and sites to visit, including the catacombs. While making the pilgrimage to Rome and the Vatican, you can obtain nourishment at some of the best restaurants in the world and sample some great red wines.

78. Make a Pilgrimage to Fatima

In 1917 Mary appeared to some children several times in Fatima, Portugal. She asked for prayers because the First World War was raging and Russia was becoming an atheistic, Communist state. The first apparition was on May 13, and subsequent apparitions were on the thirteenth of the month through October 1917. Devotion to Our Lady of Fatima began soon thereafter, and in 1930 the apparitions were declared supernatural and authentic by the Vatican. The site of the apparition draws throngs of worshipers and pilgrims.

On May 13, 1981, the anniversary of the first Fatima appearance of Our Lady, a would-be assassin shot Pope John Paul II. The pope attributed his survival to Our Lady of Fatima, and his devotion to her deepened. He publicly forgave the assassin and placed the bullet that was removed from his body in the crown on the statue commemorating Our Lady of Fatima.

Mary was said to have given the children three "secrets." The first two were revealed by one of the children after she had become a nun, Sister Lucia. The first was a gory and horrible vision of hell, a vision to scare, yes, the hell out of you. The second was a prediction of the end of World War I and the beginning of World War II, plus an exhortation to pray for the conversion of atheistic Russia.

The third secret got a lot of attention because it was a secret for a very long time. Sister Lucia wrote it down and hid it away, and the speculation on what was in it became wild and fantastic. When the secret was eventually revealed long after Sister Lucia's death, it turned out to be a mystical and apocalyptic statement, not a prediction of future events. Pope Benedict XVI wrote a treatise downplaying the secret as a fortune-teller's pronouncement. Many people were disappointed.

A personal or group pilgrimage to Fatima is something devout Catholics should consider. But prayers before a statue of Our Lady will do very well also.

79. Make a Pilgrimage to Lourdes

Another popular destination for Catholic pilgrims is Lourdes in the south of France. In February 1858 Our Lady appeared there to a teenager, Bernadette Soubirous. Bernadette was the only person who could see and communicate with the apparition, which occurred many times during the next two weeks. The Blessed Virgin asked that a chapel be built and that people should come to pray to her. There was a muddy pool in the grotto where the apparitions occurred, and Mary told Bernadette to drink and wash in a spring. Then a spring appeared from under a rock, and clear water flowed freely and in volume.

Bernadette's experience and trances attracted much attention locally, then throughout France. The local bishop declared her visions authentic and urged the faithful to come to Lourdes. Pilgrims came to pray to the Holy Mother and to drink and to bathe in the waters for cures from various ailments. When people reported miraculous cures, thousands began to come annually, then millions. In accordance with Our Lady's instruction to Bernadette, a church was built over the site. The healing waters of Lourdes continue to attract millions from around the world.

The story of Bernadette Soubirous and Our Lady of Lourdes was made into a book, a play, and then a movie: *The Song of Bernadette*. The author, Franz Werfel, was a German Jew who managed to escape to America in 1940. He wrote the story in fulfillment of a promise if he managed to avoid Nazi persecution.

Lourdes remains a popular pilgrimage destination in the twenty-first century, even for Catholics who are not seeking cures. If you cannot make it to Lourdes in your lifetime, at least stop in a church dedicated to Our Lady of Lourdes for prayer and meditation.

80. Make a Pilgrimage to Santiago de Compostela

Here's a very old, still very popular pilgrimage for Catholics. According to legend, the body of the Apostle St. James, *Santiago* in Spanish, was brought from the Holy Land to Compostela in the Galicia region of Spain in the year 813. Part of the legend is that St. James himself had been to Spain to preach and convert in Apostolic times. He was martyred when he returned to Jerusalem.

Which St. James? Catholics savvy in church history know that there were two apostles named James. Santiago was the one known as St. James the Great or St. James Major. The other James was given the unfortunate moniker of St. James the Less or St. James Minor. Thus there were apostles who might have been called colloquially "Big Jim" and "Little Jim."

The pilgrimage to the cathedral at Santiago de Compostela, if done fully, is a long walk across a good chunk of Europe. There are many routes of the *Camino de Santiago*—or St. James's Way or St. James's Route or *Le Chemin de St. Jacques*. The most popular starts in southwestern France and goes west through northern Spain to Galicia. There are many other routes, and the adventurous with lots of time can begin the journey in Geneva, Switzerland. The long walk opens time for reflection, self-examination, and interaction with other pilgrims, who come from all over the world and may not be Catholic or even Christian.

The pilgrimage is so popular that tour companies sell packages of different routes with varying degrees of accommodations. Serious pilgrims—that is, those with lots of time—will make the trek on foot and stay in hostels and inns along the way, mingling with multinational pilgrims speaking an assortment of languages.

Those who reach the cathedral after the long hike find that they have learned something about themselves and their relationship to God. Thus the pilgrimage achieves what it is supposed to do. It's been doing that for more than a thousand years.

81. Make a Pilgrimage to the Holy Land

Jerusalem! The ultimate pilgrimage. Walk, talk, and pray where Jesus, the apostles, and legions of crusaders, saints, prophets, and pilgrims walked, talked, and prayed. Planning a trip to the Holy Land can invoke anxiety because Jerusalem is perceived to be an unstable and violent city. It's true that the city is divided politically into Israeli and Palestinian sections. It is also true that there are jealousy and squabbles among Christian denominations as to which gets jurisdiction over the sites believed to be places where Jesus taught, was crucified, was buried. If thinking about going to Jerusalem makes you anxious, remember what Jesus was thinking about. He was so anxious he sweated blood in the garden of Gethsemane. Jerusalem was a lot more dangerous for him than for modern pilgrims.

While in Jerusalem, a Catholic pilgrim should also visit Judaism's holiest site, the Western Wall, also called the Wailing Wall. It is what was left after the destruction of Judaism's holiest temple. Jesus was a Jew too and may have worshiped and taught in that temple before the Romans destroyed it in A.D. 70.

Remember the story of Jesus taking up a stick and driving

the money-changers and the pigeon-sellers out of the Temple? He was appalled at the sacrilege and turned their tables over. One wonders what Jesus would do today if he wandered through Jerusalem and saw the kitsch souvenirs for sale and heard the bickering between Christian sects and between Jews and Muslims. Some tables are liable to be flipped over again.

Other places in the Holy Land are on the pilgrim's route. Bethlehem is not far from Jerusalem. To the north are the Jordan River, flowing from the Sea of Galilee, a.k.a. Lake of Gennesaret, south to the Dead Sea; and Cana and Nazareth, west of the Sea of Galilee.

Dozens of tour companies sell many different tours of the Holy Land. Think about your reaction to walking where Jesus and his apostles walked.

82. Participate in the C.Y.O.

Every Catholic knows this acronym-abbreviation: the "See-Why-O." But do you remember what it stands for? In some large American dioceses, the C.Y.O. is a big deal. It organizes, usually at the parish level, spiritual, athletic, and cultural events for young Catholics, adolescents and young adults, hence its full name, "Catholic Youth Organization." The mission of the C.Y.O. is straightforward: to help form young people into responsible adult Catholics and Catholic leaders committed to the teaching and example of Jesus Christ.

Some large parishes have very active C.Y.O. branches, with athletic leagues made up of other C.Y.O. branches in other parishes. There are seminars, social events, liturgy, and service projects. The C.Y.O. members participate in World Youth Day. At such an event, they may even get to meet the pope. The C.Y.O. helps needy people, provides outreach to at-risk children, and evangelizes at a personal level.

Even if you are no longer of the age to be considered a "young" adult, you can and should participate in the C.Y.O. Adult leaders are necessary for the organization to achieve its mission and goals. Are you a wannabe coach whose playing days are in the past? Suck in your gut, hang a whistle around your neck, get back out on the field, and coach C.Y.O. sports teams. Lots of adults know that working with teenagers and young adults is a good way to stay connected across generations and to share their own knowledge and enthusiasm.

Catholicism isn't static; it needs committed adults to pass it on to those coming up.

83. Give Necco Wafers to Children

Fake Mass may seem irreverent, sacrilegious to Catholics who think humor is incompatible with being a good Christian, but that no-fun attitude is more in line with traditional Calvinism than with Catholicism. Who didn't, as a child, eat Necco Wafers while pretending to say Mass? The candy is just about the same size and shape as the unleavened bread wafers used in celebrating the Eucharist and Holy Communion. Actually, this practice should be encouraged in children because, not only is it not irreverent, it teaches and reminds them about the rituals of Mass and receiving Holy Communion.

Set up a play altar, put some sort of shawl or robe on the boys, and let them be mini-priests for the moment. They can break out the Necco Wafers and distribute them to the other children. This is a good opportunity for the adults to remind the children of the significance of Holy Communion. Children are smart enough to understand the difference between play-acting and the real event. Besides, an adult can get in the make-believe communion line too, pop a Necco Wafer into the mouth, and generate a memory of childhood.

Necco Wafers: they're not just for Halloween trick-or-treat.

84. Use Home Candles

The fire marshal probably doesn't approve, but burning blessed candles in the home is an old tradition. The tradition was to bring candles to church on Candlemas, February 2, and have them blessed along with those to be used in the church itself. These home candles are used on the Advent wreath, for holiday celebrations, and during family prayer sessions. There is an old practice, more superstition than devotion, to light blessed candles during a storm for protection.

Home candles are especially appropriate when a sick or elderly family member is too frail to leave the house and go to church. When the Eucharistic Minister or deacon comes with Holy Communion, greeting that person with a lighted blessed candle and escorting him or her to the disabled family member is the proper devotional procedure. The same can be said if a priest comes to administer the sacrament of the Anointing of the Sick.

Just because a candle is blessed and is used sacramentally or liturgically does not mean that it can't start a fire. Fire marshals and home casualty insurers would prefer if homeowners never burn candles for any purpose. There is a substitute, however. They're called electric candles. It's OK to use electric and LED candles as part of home worship and devotion. It's safer too. The purpose of the candle is to call attention to the prayer accompanying it, the flame representing the light of Christ. Although LED candles don't have the traditional panache of wax candles, their use at home is appropriate for safety. If you use wax candles in your home for whatever reason, do not leave them unattended. Even blessed candles can burn your house down.

85. Participate in Catholic Schools

There is a persistent mythical image of a Catholic school. The girls are in pleated-skirt uniforms, the boys in khaki or gray. A nun in full habit stands in front of the class with a ruler or yardstick, unsmiling, ready and willing to inflict corporal punishment on misbehavers. There's a lot more to Catholic education than that.

Besides grade schools, there are hundreds of Catholic high schools throughout the U.S. If you didn't do elementary and secondary education at a Catholic school, there are dozens of colleges and universities that are identified as Catholic. Some are well known, like Notre Dame in Indiana and Georgetown and Catholic University in Washington, D.C. There are four universities named "Loyola": Los Angeles, Chicago, New Orleans, and Baltimore. (The Jesuits like to honor their founder, St. Ignatius of Loyola.) There are three named "Xavier": Cincinnati, Chicago, and New Orleans. Other Catholic colleges and universities get attention during basketball season, especially if their teams are doing well. Think: Creighton, St. Bonaventure, Villanova.

Even if you didn't go to Catholic elementary or high school or a Catholic college, you can still be part of the large Catholic schools network. Most Catholic colleges offer on-line courses, non-credit courses, lectures, theater, and concerts that are open to the public. Catholics should take advantage of these opportunities. Many Catholic elementary and high schools welcome participation by volunteers even if there is no connection to the school, such as being a parent or an alumnus. Reading, mathematics, and homework tutors assist struggling students to keep up their grades. And, as with most Catholic institutions, participation in the mission and operation of the schools through monetary contributions is always encouraged.

86. Teach C.C.D. Classes

For students not attending Catholic schools, Catholic education is achieved through the program known as C.C.D. Do you remember—that is, if you ever knew—what those initials stand for? In the standard practice of Catholic Church officialdom of using elaborate, even pompous, terms to describe something simple and straightforward, the program of providing instruction in Catholicism to elementary and secondary students is called the Confraternity of Christian Doctrine, C.C.D. for short.

Each parish has a program in which students come to the parish center, the school, or the church, once a week usually, to learn about the Catholic Church and what it means to be a Catholic. This is what the Protestant churches usually call "Sunday School." C.C.D. classes are not necessarily held on Sunday, although it is common practice for the instruction to be done just before or immediately after Sunday Mass. Some parishes have the C.C.D. classes on weekday evenings; it all depends on local practice and tradition.

You can help educate young Catholics about the basics of their religion. The C.C.D. programs all rely on volunteer teachers. You'll be given materials to prepare the classes, and the students will have the necessary books. C.C.D. is the opportunity to pass on your Faith and devotion to the next generation. Get yourself a copy of *The Catechism of the Catholic Church* and brush up on topics such as sanctifying grace, the seven sacraments, transubstantiation, and apostolic succession. You will have the opportunity to explain what it means when you recite the Nicene Creed every Sunday and use the phrase "consubstantial with the Father." Be prepared for some interesting and challenging questions and a rewarding experience.

87. Lift a Toast with Catholic Liquor

The next time you're in your local liquor store, go to the section with brandies and liqueurs and check out the Catholic titles. You will find made-in-America Christian Brothers brandy, popular and inexpensive. Until the late 1980s the brandy and some table wines were made by the Christian Brothers in their vineyard and winery in California's Napa Valley. The brothers got out of the booze business then, and they sold the winery and the name to a company that continues to make brandy but no wine.

In the liqueur section there are liqueurs made by monks in Europe. The herb-infused, green or yellow Chartreuse is aromatic and potent, containing 130 different herbs, plants, and flowers. It was created hundreds of years ago as a tonic, a medicine, an elixir, but the high alcohol content made its purported therapeutic benefits moot. The Carthusian monks of France continue to manufacture it, supporting their monasteries and spreading joy to all who sip it.

The myth of the liqueur called "Benedictine" is that it was created by French Benedictine monks as a medicinal tonic like Chartreuse. Not so. The cozy story about the monks was created as a marketing ploy by the layman who developed the intricate blend of flavors. When you drink it, you can pretend that French monks made it.

Monks do make a lot of beer. The Trappist monks have several breweries throughout the world and carefully guard the use of the "Trappist" label on beers. The Trappist monks' beer is so good that competitors sometimes use the term "monk" on their labels. Don't be misled! Accept no substitutes! Check the label to see if the beer is brewed in a monastery brewery by real monks.

Lift a toast to the holy men who guard the Catholic tradition of fine beer and liqueurs.

88. Visit a Monastery

The Trappist monks make a lot more than beer. The rules of religious orders dedicated to St. Benedict require each monastery to be self-sufficient. Many of the Trappist monasteries in the United States were once farms where cows were milked and chickens laid eggs. The changes in commercial agriculture made such relatively small monastic operations unprofitable, and the monks found new ways to support themselves. The well-known Abbey of Our Lady of Gethsemani is a good example. The monks there operate an on-site and on-line store selling specialty foods and candies, such as preserves and fudge. Best known is their fruitcake, which is saturated with Kentucky bourbon whiskey, appropriate inasmuch as the monastery is located in Kentucky.

Other monasteries welcome visitors for guided spiritual retreats and conferences. St. Joseph's Abbey, a Benedictine monastery near Covington, Louisiana, houses a minor seminary, the first step in young men's development toward becoming priests. The monks also have a workshop where they make wooden coffins for sale to the public. Many monasteries have a shop attached where spiritual items, gifts, and souvenirs are sold. The Abbey of New Clairvaux in Northern California operates a farm growing plums, grapes, and walnuts.

Catholics can easily get acquainted with the world of monks and monasticism by attending Mass with the monks. Don't

expect a quick in and out for Sunday Mass. After all, the life of the monks is, according to St. Benedict's rule, prayer and work (*ora et labora*). The monk's day is filled with both, giving him little time for distraction and temptation. At least that's the idea of the rule. The monks usually welcome laypeople at their liturgies, but call or check the monastery's website before going.

89. Look Up Your Patron Saints

Do you know your patron saint? At Baptism, every Catholic is given a name of a saint. The name may also be a family tradition, and there are so many saints that it's easy to find a name that is agreeable. By the time Catholics become adults, a lot of us have forgotten about the saint behind our names. For women named Mary, Maria, Marie, or Marian, it's easy to remember that you were named for the Blessed Mother. The same goes for men named Joseph. Some names refer to many different saints. For example, if your name is John, there are many saints by that name for whom you may have been named. The obvious are St. John the Baptist and St. John the Apostle. There are saints named John of

the Cross, John Chrysostom, John Henry Newman, Pope John XXIII, John Damascene, John Bosco, and even St. John the Dwarf. Look up your patron saint in the *Catholic Encyclopedia* or in a book of saints. You can also look up the patron saint of your city or other geographical location. Many places in the United States are named for saints, a common practice of the French and Spanish colonists: St. Paul, Minnesota; San Antonio, Texas; St. Augustine, Florida; St. Joseph, Missouri; Santa Clara, California; and a lot more.

Your occupation or profession probably has a patron saint, whose history you can read about. St. Peter is the patron of fishermen and St. Matthew the patron of I.R.S. tax collectors. St. Lucy is the patron of everything to do with eyes. St. Raymond of Penyafort is patron of medical records librarians, and St. Caecilia is the patron of musicians. There is even a patron saint of coffeehouse keepers, St. Drogo. Catholicism has a patron saint for everybody, no matter what they do, including nothing at all. (St. Cajetan is the patron of the unemployed.)

Look up your patron saints; it's interesting and inspiring.

90. Attend a Latin Mass

"Give Me That Old Time Religion!" That hymn goes back to the American Protestant churches in the nineteenth century, but Old Time Catholic religion is a lot older. Although Latin was not the language of Jesus, it was the language of the early Church. In the fourth century, St. Jerome translated the Bible from various forms of literary Latin and Greek into a simple form of Latin that was easily understood. Latin became and remained the official language of the Church.

The Second Vatican Council in the 1960s allowed, encouraged, mandated that Mass be celebrated in vernacular languages. The use of Latin fell away; seminaries stopped requiring future priests to study the language. Nostalgia and an appreciation for the elegant solemnity of the old Latin Mass kept it alive, and some parish churches, especially those with an influential traditionalist congregation and pastor, lobbied their bishops to allow the old form of the Mass, in Latin, to be celebrated on occasion. The practice has grown, and most dioceses will allow Latin Mass as long as there is a priest trained and approved to recite the liturgy in the old language.

If you have never attended a Mass in Latin, doing so should be on your list. Most inspiring is a solemn high Mass in the old Tridentine ritual, with the priest facing the altar. The choir and the congregation will chant the *Kyrie Eleison* (which is Greek, not Latin), the *Gloria in Excelsis Deo,* and the Nicene Creed (*"Credo"*) in Gregorian chant. Most churches that have Latin Masses will have booklets available for the congregation to follow at least part of the liturgy. After a couple of Latin Masses during which you paid careful attention, you should be able to recite the Lord's Prayer in Latin: *"Pater noster qui es in caelis . . . "*

91. Celebrate Mass in a Foreign Language

One of the characteristics of the Catholic Church is that it is truly catholic (lowercase c). That means that it is universal, welcoming all nationalities and languages. Does your parish schedule Masses in a language other than English? If so, participate, at least passively, in the liturgy in a different language or for a different ethnic group. English didn't even exist in Jesus' day, and the first Mass, the Last Supper, was probably in Old Aramaic.

Many dioceses in the United States have parishes that celebrate Mass in a variety of languages. The largest, the Archdiocese of Los Angeles, includes churches that regularly have Mass in dozens of different languages and rites, all as part of the universal Catholic Church. From Arabic and Armenian to Samoan, Thai, and Ukrainian, there are churches in and around L.A. where you can experience some rather exotic (to Americans) expressions of devotion.

If you want to attend Mass celebrated in the language of Jesus (almost), look up a church that uses the Syro-Malabar Rite. Some of the services may be conducted in Syriac, a language closer to the Aramaic that Jesus spoke. The Syro-Malabar Rite includes several million Catholics in India and Indian communities in the United States. They have their own American diocese, St. Thomas Syro-Malabar Diocese of Chicago, with more than thirty churches throughout the United States. Have you ever heard hymns being sung in Hindi? Check with a Syro-Malabar church near you and experience a form of worship that will enhance your appreciation of the catholicity of Catholicism.

There are probably other foreign-language churches closer to you, so plan to attend a Mass in Spanish on the Feast of Our Lady of Guadalupe, December 12, or in Polish on the Feast of St. John Paul II, October 22.

92. Participate in a Red Mass

"Red" was once a pejorative term for Leftists, Marxists, Communists, and their "fellow travelers." The word describes anger: "seeing red." More recently, it has been used to describe a U.S. state with a majority of the voters belonging to the Republican Party.

For hundreds of years in Catholicism, the term "Red Mass" has been used to describe a special Mass celebrated to invoke the intercession of the Holy Spirit on everyone involved in the legal process: judges, lawyers, legislators, law students, etc. The name comes from the color of the vestments worn, red being the color of the Mass of the Holy Spirit on one of the most solemn feasts on the church calendar, Pentecost.

The Red Mass is usually organized in a diocese by the local chapter of the St. Thomas More Catholic Lawyers Society. St. Thomas More, patron saint of lawyers, was a brilliant Catholic lawyer, theologian, philosopher, and adviser to King Henry VIII. When King Henry and Thomas had a disagreement that reached an impasse, Thomas lost his head, literally, at the king's direction. (At this point, readers can insert an appropriate—or inappropriate—lawyer joke.) St. Thomas More was canonized as a martyr.

Depending on local practice, before the Red Mass begins, members of the judiciary will process into the church or cathedral in robes, much like a graduation ceremony minus the mortarboard hats. The public is welcome and invited to participate, not the least important reason being that lawyers and judges need all the prayer they can get.

Inquire at your local diocese's office for when the Red Mass will be celebrated. Many dioceses schedule the Red Mass on the first Monday in October, the day the U.S. Supreme Court and many other courts officially open the judicial year. No lawyer jokes during Mass, please.

93. Pray the Angelus

At 6:00 A.M., noon, and 6:00 P.M., it is time to pray the Angelus. The prayer is a group effort, sort of a call-and-response, but saying it alone is theologically fine too. It recalls the experience of Mary when she was greeted by the Angel Gabriel and informed that she was to be the mother of the Messiah. The event is known as the Annunciation.

The Angelus is a very old devotion. Its practice goes back at least to the fourteenth century, when there were no clocks and ordinary life was rural and plain. In the morning the church bell would toll to begin the workday. At noon the bell would signal the sun crossing the meridian and the time for a repast. The evening bell would mark the end of the workday. On each occasion the faithful would pause to recite the short prayer acknowledging Mary's acceptance of her role and her impregnation by the power of the Holy Spirit. Modern Catholics continue the practice, although not necessarily at six, noon, and six every day.

Versicle: The angel of the Lord declared unto Mary;
Response: And she conceived of the Holy Spirit.
(Hail, Mary, full of grace . . .)

And so forth.

The Angelus is known to many Catholics and non-Catholics alike through an 1859 painting by the French artist Jean-François Millet. It shows a couple in a field with agricultural implements, bowed in prayer, almost in silhouette as the ambient light is either early morning or dusk or cloudy or a manifestation of Millet's vision of the event. To millions who have seen the painting, *The Angelus* is no more than the title of a fine work of art. To practicing Catholics, it is a reminder of the prayer acknowledging one of the most significant events in Christian theology.

94. Schedule a Blessing of the Animals

Even many atheists know that St. Francis of Assisi is the patron saint of animals. He is the best known and most loved of the saints because of his gentleness, his mystical and intense devotion. Many legends about Francis focus on his love of animals and birds. Such an aura he carried with him that the creatures of the world responded to him when he spoke to them. (Francis was a little weird.) Francis lived in thirteenth-century Italy, and his influence on Catholicism and the Church was immediate, profound, and lasting. The order he founded, the Franciscans,

National Gallery of Art, Washington, Gallery Archives

spreads its presence and influence throughout the world today. Francis became the patron saint of animals because of the stories about him, whether they were factually accurate or not. He is often depicted surrounded by birds and animals. Yard statuary of Francis is popular, especially of him holding a bowl in front of him that becomes a birdbath.

Many parishes and dioceses honor St. Francis with a ceremony of the blessing of the animals, just as Francis had done 800 years ago. Catholics and non-Catholics alike bring their pets and other animals to a location where a priest offers prayers and blesses the animals to show that they are worthy of love, just as Francis showed them. Police on horseback are there; service animals to be sure are welcome, but so are coops and cages with hamsters and gerbils, cockatoos and canaries, bunnies and guinea pigs, and squirming and mewing cats and frisky dogs. The Franciscan blessing is pronounced over them, they are sprinkled with holy water, and they are recognized as blessed creatures of God.

If your parish or diocese doesn't have a Blessing of the Animals day, schedule one and see all the people and pets who will show up. The Feast Day of St. Francis is October 4, a good day to set the event.

95. Say Grace Before Meals

One of the most recognized paintings by Norman Rockwell is titled *Saying Grace.* Rockwell was a master of scenes of ordinary Americans in their daily lives. In his 1951 painting a boy and an older woman sit in a crowded restaurant, sharing a table with a couple of rough-looking dudes, one of whom dangles a cigarette from his lips as the men stare at their devout table-sharers. The woman and the boy have clasped hands and bowed heads as they remember to give thanks before eating.

The Catholic Grace Before Meals is one of the earliest prayers children learn, possibly because it is so easy to remember. The simple prayer gets right to the point, food, and becomes fixed in memory for a lifetime. All Catholics regularly use it—or should. In fact, it is so simple, easy, and devout that many non-Catholic Christians use it too.

Bless us, O Lord, and these thy gifts, which we are about to

receive from thy bounty, through Christ our Lord. Amen. (It's OK to use "your" in place of "thy." You don't have to pray like a Quaker.)

Catholic children are taught at home and in school that if the setting for the meal is public or noisy or otherwise awkward for an outward display of reverence, grace should be said silently, mentally. The whole purpose is to put oneself in the presence of God and acknowledge that God is the provider of all things.

Art collectors and dealers should give thanks too. The original of Rockwell's painting has sold for millions of dollars.

96. Offer a Prayer on Game Day

The Hail Mary is the prayer most recognized as being unique to Catholicism. Despite—or perhaps because of—the stilted English translation of *Ave Maria, gratia plena* . . . it is a prayer recited regularly by Catholics. Every complete recitation of the rosary includes fifty-three repetitions of the prayer. Even though the prayer has no specific request other than "pray for us, sinners . . . " it is routinely recited when a heavenly favor is requested. Hence its entry into the hackneyed jargon of football for a forward pass that is thrown in controlled desperation, hoping that the right player on the right team will catch it in the right place.

Holy Mother Mary did not, of course, know anything of football. This fact does not deter anyone from implying that one of those forward passes will somehow be guided by her intercession. Has anyone considered that Mary may know nothing of football, may not care, or may be a fan of the defensive team?

There are specifically designated patron saints of athletics, and, if someone wants to invoke their intercession, they may be more appropriate. St. Sebastian, a third-century martyr, is the designated patron of athletes. It is unclear why, but an unhistorical legend is that Sebastian was martyred by archers shooting arrows into him. A better choice would be nineteenth-century St. Luigi Scrosoppi, the patron of "footballers," *i.e.*, soccer players. True, there are no "Hail Mary" passes in soccer. Don't expect television commentators to refer to a desperate forward pass as a "Luigi" or a "Scrosoppi," but you can offer a prayer to him anyway.

Catholic and other Christian schools use the mascot name of "Saints." And the National Football League has a whole team of them, the New Orleans Saints. The fans of these teams may or may not be voicing a theological exhortation when they call out, "Go, Saints!"

97. Visit the Dead on All Saints Day

This is another feast day that creeps up on many Catholics. It's usually on a weekday, and it is the day after Halloween. You look at the calendar and say something like, "Uh-oh, another holy day of obligation," then start feeling uneasy because you don't know whether you can make it to Mass.

Halloween and All Saints Day go together. Halloween is a squeezed-in version of "All Hallows Eve," that is, the evening before the Feast of All Hallows, an old name for All Saints Day. The feast day may have been instituted to counter the Celtic festival of Samhain on October 31, which celebrated dead ancestors. The popularity of Halloween in contemporary culture, with its ghosts and goblins and ghouls, has overshadowed All Saints Day to the point that it begins to look as though the pagans have returned full strength.

In some ethnic cultures, All Saints Day is observed by visits to the tombs and graves of loved ones, where prayers are recited for the dead and flowers are placed on the burial sites. Weather permitting, some dioceses authorize the celebration of Mass in the cemeteries themselves. Worshipers can fulfill their holy day responsibility and visit their dead loved ones at the same time.

Take advantage of the opportunity, if it's available, to hear Mass in a graveyard. Even if there is no Mass being offered, you should visit dead relatives and friends to connect with them in memory and prayer. Just think, old Uncle Julius, God bless his soul, who was always such a pain at family Thanksgiving dinners, might be surprised that you would be stopping by his grave with a bouquet of flowers.

98. Celebrate El Dia De Los Muertos

Combining the Catholic observances of All Saints Day (November 1) and All Souls Day (November 2) with an ancient Aztec celebration, the Mexican Day of the Dead has spread well beyond Mexico. It is celebrated wherever there are expatriate Mexicans or persons of Mexican descent or others who have no Mexican connection but enjoy an excuse for an unusual party. All Souls Day is by design somber; it is a day when Catholics offer prayers for the deceased who are in Purgatory, "doing time" before they can get into heaven. They need to be cheered up, and combining All Saints Day with All Souls Day with the cultural adhesive of an ancient folk festival takes care of that.

Grinning skulls are everywhere! The grin is not something grim but joyful, even mischievous. The spirit of *El Dia De Los Muertos* is that the dead are having a good time, being entertained by the living. This is no different from the European way of observing All Saints Day with flowers and visits to ancestors' burial sites. Who said being dead had to be dark and glum?

If you have never been to a celebration of *El Dia De Los Muertos,* you should check out what may be going on in your city or nearby. Typically there is a carnival atmosphere, with food and drinks and lots of specially made candy that resembles skulls. Even people who are not religious will have an altar in their home decorated for the day and dedicated to deceased family and friends.

In some communities there will be public parades and display altars on streets and in parks. The Day of the Dead should be on your list, because it is a way of participating in a folk expression of Catholic belief that goes beyond a recitation in the Nicene Creed of a belief in "the resurrection of the dead."

99. Play Bingo!

What? You don't play bingo?! How can you call yourself a Catholic? Before the casinos and the lotteries took over what is euphemistically called the "gaming" industry, the only legal places for games of chance were private clubs and Catholic parish halls. Bingo games were part of the support of the parish school and other programs. School cafeterias often one night a week echoed with the rattle of the bingo balls in the caller's basket and the cries of "O twenty-nine" and "G fourteen" until one of the participants would jump up in glee, yell, "Bingo!" and claim the jackpot.

Bingo wasn't just for bored old people with nothing better to do. Families with children participated too because everyone knew that the proceeds were for a good cause. Buy a bingo card or two and, even if you didn't win anything, the money spent went to the parish or the school.

Then the public rules on bingo were relaxed, and bingo parlors appeared in civic clubs and then in private, for-profit bingo halls. The lottery and the casinos drew off the true gamblers who had

heretofore attempted to assuage their compulsions at church-run bingo. It was always an uneasy understanding that betting in the form of bingo supported the local Catholic church. This drew the ire of surrounding conservative Protestant denominations, for whom gambling was a serious sin on the level with drinking and card-playing.

Still, bingo survives in some Catholic parishes and for the same reasons it always has. For some people it is much easier to drop a few bucks on bingo boards than to deposit an equal amount in the collection basket during Sunday Mass.

If you have never been to a Catholic church bingo night, search one out and experience what may seem to be a walk through a time warp. While playing bingo, it's best not to meditate on the scene in the New Testament where the Roman soldiers are shooting dice for Jesus' clothes while he is hanging on the cross. "Bingo!"

100. Receive the Anointing of the Sick

The last of the seven sacraments was once called "The Last Rites" or "Extreme Unction." A person facing death or with a serious, life-threatening illness was anointed with holy oil, and special prayers were said to soothe the afflicted person and to ease the entry of the soul into heaven after death. If the recipient were physically able, she or he received Holy Communion in a rite called "Viaticum," Latin for "take it with you along the way," nourishment for the journey to heaven. The "unction" is the holy oil, and "extreme" means it is done at the end of life.

The theology was modified in the Second Vatican Council, and the sacrament became the "Anointing of the Sick," and it was no longer restricted to those who were in danger of immediate death. Today the sacrament is administered to those who face serious threat to their health, even if they are not in predictable danger of expiring.

If you or someone close to you fits into the described category, call the priest and arrange for the sacrament. Hospital and hospice chaplains anoint sick people regularly, but it can be

Photograph by Anne Renouf, courtesy of the Jubilee Museum, Columbus, Ohio

done in the home or any place where a person is seriously sick or facing death. Priests sometimes arrive at the scenes of serious accidents to minister to the badly injured. Military chaplains have administered the Last Rites on the battlefield.

You're at the end of your list, the journey through *100 Catholic Things to Do Before You Die*. You've received the Last Rites, the Anointing of the Sick. You can now lie down and die. If you've done everything right, you'll go to heaven, soon. Make the Sign of the Cross, and close this book.

Requiescat in pace. Rest in peace.

Amen.

Index